THE AUSTRALIAN
Women's Weekly
super diet

acp books

CONTENTS

EAT WELL LOOK GOOD

NO MATTER WHAT THEY TELL YOU, LOTIONS, POTIONS AND SERUMS ARE NOT THE ANSWER TO NATURAL BEAUTY. THE BEST RECIPE FOR LOOKING GOOD IS LOTS OF FRESH FRUIT AND VEGETABLES, PLENTY OF WATER AND MOVING YOUR BODY. EATING FRIED FOODS AND DRINKING COLA IS NEVER GOING TO GIVE YOU SHINY HAIR AND GLOWING SKIN, JUST AS EXTREME DIETING ISN'T THE WAY TO HEALTHY BONES AND STRONG NAILS. IF YOU WANT TO SLOW DOWN THE AGEING PROCESS AND LOOK GOOD, FOLLOW THESE SIMPLE TIPS TO GET YOUR BEAUTY RADIATING FROM THE INSIDE OUT.

NUTRITION FOR YOUR HAIR AND NAILS

A DIET FULL OF A VARIETY OF VITAMINS AND MINERALS IS THE KEY TO KEEPING YOUR HAIR AND NAILS IN TIP-TOP SHAPE.

• Our hair is made up of 97% protein, so eat lots of high-quality protein foods for healthy shiny hair. Find protein in nuts, lean meats, seafood and eggs.

• Calcium is vital for hair and nail growth. Get your daily dose from low-fat dairy foods like yogurt and reduced-fat cheese.

• Zinc is an essential mineral and powerful antioxidant found in oysters, red meats, beans and wholegrains. It promotes cell production, tissue growth and plays a vital role in collagen formation, which means it's also great for your complexion.

• Iron deficiency has been shown to promote hair loss. Keep baldness at bay by increasing your iron intake with red meat and green leafy vegetables.

• Prevent hair and nail breakage by eating silicon-rich foods such as onions, broccoli, cabbage, fish, strawberries and oats. Silicon stimulates cell metabolism and cell growth, which means it's great at repairing damaged skin.

MOVE YOUR BODY

HEALTHY SKIN IS BOOSTED BY GOOD CIRCULATION AND THE FLUSHING OUT OF TOXINS. NOTHING GETS THE HEART PUMPING AND THE BODY SWEATING BETTER THAN REGULAR EXERCISE. IT DOESN'T NEED TO BE DRAMATIC, JUST AS LONG AS IT'S CONSTANT: SO GET MOVING.

• Find an activity that you enjoy whether it's dancing, boating or walking your dog. The more distracted you are by having fun, the less likely you are to lose interest.

• Don't underestimate the power of incidental exercise. Taking the stairs instead of the lift or hopping off the bus earlier are both painless ways you can incorporate extra exercise into your day.

• Stretching is a fantastic way to tone and condition your muscles. The stronger your muscles are, the firmer and more beautiful the skin attached to them is. Pilates and yoga are fun and gentle ways to incorporate stretching into your routine.

MAKE FRIENDS WITH FATS

PLUMP UP YOUR SKIN WITHOUT PLUMPING UP THE REST OF YOU. KNOWING YOUR GOOD FATS FROM YOUR BAD FATS IS ESSENTIAL FOR YOUTHFUL LOOKING SKIN.

• For maximum skin boosting impact, eat oily fish like salmon and ocean trout, 2-3 times a week. They're full of omega-3 fatty acids that keep the skin supple and wrinkle-free.
• Nuts keep our skin young and radiant thanks to their good oils and vitamins. Different nuts are good for different things. Almonds are packed with calcium, iron, protein and fibre to maintain a healthy digestive system. Walnuts are full of omega-3s, copper and magnesium for healthy skin and bones. Brazil nuts house powerful antioxidants that combat free radical molecules that make skin dry, wrinkly and dull. Limit yourself to 30g of nuts a day and make sure to mix them up. There is so much variety you'd be nuts not to try them all.
• Avocados keep your skin moist and soft thanks to a fat called oleic acid. They're also packed full of vitamin E, which increases the growth of new skin cells. As an added bonus, avocados make a great pumice stone substitute: rub the inside of the skin on your heels to get rid of dry skin.

FILL UP ON FLAVOUR

PEOPLE THINK THAT TRIMMING THE FAT OFF MEAT AND REDUCING SALT EQUATES TO FLAVOURLESS FOOD, BUT THAT'S NOT THE CASE. GIVE THESE FLAVOUR-BOOSTING ALTERNATIVES A TRY, AND YOU'LL NEVER MISS THE SALT.

• Add spices, fresh herbs, garlic and ginger, a little wine, flavoured vinegars, fresh lemon or lime juice, lemon grass or chillies, etc.
• Sprinkle nuts and seeds over sweet or savoury dishes to add taste and texture.
• Keeping your body hydrated is essential for clear skin. Make water more appealing with a squeeze of lemon, a sprig of mint and some freshly sliced cucumber.
• Ditch the sugar and opt for natural sweeteners like honey or puréed fruit. You won't notice the difference but your body will.

FRUIT AND VEGIES: YOUR NEW BEST FRIENDS

THEY'RE PACKED FULL OF GOODIES SO EAT THEM RAW IF YOU CAN, IF NOT, COOK THEM SIMPLY AND FAST.

• Eat a variety of colours. The more colourful your plate the more vitamins, minerals and antioxidants are at work to have you looking wonderful.
• Always buy fruit and vegies in small amounts. If they've been sitting in the fridge all week they'll lose colour, flavour and nutritional goodness.

THE ELITE ANTI-AGEING FRUIT AND VEGIE GROUP

BERRIES ARE ANTI-AGEING SUPER-STARS PACKED WITH VITAMIN C AND POWERFUL ANTIOXIDANTS; SPRINKLE THEM ON YOUR PORRIDGE OR EAT FROZEN BERRIES AS A SUMMER SNACK.

• Prevent cell ageing with tomatoes. They contain lipocene, an antioxidant and anti-cancer agent. The raw rule needn't apply here. Cooking tomatoes produces five times more lipocene than if you eat them raw. So whip up a big batch of guilt-free pasta sauce.
• Green leafy vegies like broccoli and spinach cleanse the liver to keep blood flowing and skin glowing. They also contain coenzyme Q10, which is a popular ingredient in anti-ageing moisturisers. Why spend the money on expensive moisturisers when you can eat them for dinner?

YOUR SKIN, HAIR AND NAILS ARE THE WINDOW TO YOUR HEALTH. NO AMOUNT OF EXPENSIVE BEAUTY PRODUCTS CAN MAKE UP FOR A POOR DIET AND SEDENTARY LIFESTYLE. REPAIR STILL OCCURS AS WE AGE, SO IT'S NEVER TOO LATE TO START EATING WELL AND LOOKING GOOD.

IN THIS BOOK WE WILL SHOW YOU HOW THE RIGHT FOODS CAN HELP TO KEEP YOU STRONG, HEALTHY AND BEAUTIFUL.

THE ALL-IMPORTANT BREAKFAST

SCRAMBLED EGGS FLORENTINE

4 eggs

6 egg whites

2 tablespoons reduced-fat milk

2 tablespoons finely chopped fresh chives

2 teaspoons vegetable oil

150g baby spinach leaves

4 slices soy-linseed bread, toasted

1 Whisk eggs, egg whites, milk and chives in medium bowl. Heat oil in large frying pan, add egg mixture; cook, stirring, over low heat until creamy.

2 Place spinach in colander over sink; pour over about 2 cups of boiling water. Drain well.

3 Serve spinach and eggs on toast.

prep + cook time *20 minutes* serves 4
nutritional count per serving 9.5g total fat
(2.3g saturated fat); 928kJ (222 cal);
15.7g carbohydrate; 17.2g protein; 2.7g fibre

A well-balanced and substantial breakfast will get you through to lunchtime. If you're really hungry around mid-morning – not just bored – eat a piece of fruit or snack lightly on dried fruit and nuts.

STRAWBERRY SOY SHAKE

Blend 125g strawberries, 1½ cups reduced-fat soy milk, 150g firm silken tofu and 1 tablespoon honey until smooth.

prep + cook time *10 minutes* serves *2*
nutritional count per serving *2.5g total fat (0.4g saturated fat); 811kJ (194 cal); 26.7g carbohydrate; 14.6g protein; 3.5g fibre*

TROPICAL FRUIT SMOOTHIE

Blend ½ cup fresh orange juice, ½ peeled and chopped small pineapple, 100ml strained passionfruit juice, 250g low-fat yogurt and 1 tablespoon wheat germ until smooth.

prep time *30 minutes* serves *2*
nutritional count per serving *0.8g total fat (0.2g saturated fat); 769kJ (184 cal); 25.3g carbohydrate; 11.1g protein; 10.1g fibre*

You need about 5 passionfruit for this recipe.

FRESH SUNRISE SMOOTHIE

Blend 1 coarsely chopped medium mango, 1 sliced medium banana, ½ cup fresh orange juice, ½ peeled and chopped small pineapple, and 1 cup rice milk until smooth.

prep time *30 minutes* serves 2
nutritional count per serving *5.1g total fat (3g saturated fat); 1304kJ (312 cal); 53.8g carbohydrate; 10g protein; 6.4g fibre*

BANANAS IN ALMOND MILK

Blend 2 tablespoons ground almonds, 2 tablespoons wheat germ and 2 tablespoons honey with 1 sliced medium banana and 1¾ cups reduced-fat soy milk until smooth.

prep time *10 minutes* serves 2
nutritional count per serving *6.1g total fat (0.4g saturated fat); 1212kJ (290 cal); 48g carbohydrate; 10.5g protein; 4.9g fibre*

GLUTEN-FREE PUFFED MUESLI

2 cups (40g) puffed brown rice

2 cups (45g) puffed corn

2 cups (30g) puffed millet

2 cups (120g) crunchy rice flakes

½ cup (80g) sultanas

½ cup (100g) pepitas

½ cup (75g) sunflower seed kernels

½ cup brazil nuts (80g), finely chopped

½ cup (55g) dried goji berries

1 Combine ingredients in large bowl; store in an airtight container.

prep time *10 minutes serves 20*
nutritional count per serving *7.2g total fat (1.1g saturated fat); 577kJ (138 cal); 14.2g carbohydrate; 3.6g protein; 2.2g fibre*

Store gluten-free puffed muesli in the fridge for 3 months.
Goji berries are small red berries that grow on a type of shrub that originated around Tibet. While often eaten dried, the berries can be eaten straight from the vine. Sweet, with a delicious flavour, dried goji berries are available in health-food stores and major supermarkets.

ROLLED BARLEY FRUIT TRIFLE

4 apricots (200g)

125g small strawberries

2 cups (560g) yogurt

½ cup (60g) rolled barley

⅓ cup (40g) LSA

1 tablespoon honey

1 Halve, stone and slice apricots thinly. Quarter strawberries; combine with apricots in small bowl.
2 Divide half the fruit between four 1½-cup (375ml) glasses. Top with half the yogurt. Spoon over barley, LSA, honey and remaining yogurt.
3 Cover glasses and remaining fruit separately; place in refrigerator overnight.
4 Top trifles with remaining fruit to serve.
prep time *15 minutes* serves *4*
nutritional count per serving *10g total fat (2.8g saturated fat); 1083kJ (259 cal); 27.2g carbohydrate; 11.8g protein; 3.6g fibre*

LSA is a mixture of ground linseeds, sunflower seed kernels and almonds; available in health-food shops or the health-food section in supermarkets.

OVEN-BAKED RÖSTI WITH BREAKFAST BEANS

1 small kumara (250g), grated coarsely

1 medium potato (200g), grated coarsely

1 teaspoon coarse cooking salt

1 egg

2 tablespoons self-raising flour

1 small red onion (100g), chopped finely

1 tablespoon vegetable oil

breakfast beans

1 tablespoon oil

1 medium brown onion (150g), sliced thinly

2 cloves garlic, crushed

400g can diced tomatoes

¼ cup (60ml) water

400g can cannellini beans, rinsed, drained

¼ cup coarsely chopped fresh flat-leaf parsley

1 Make breakfast beans.

2 Preheat oven to 200°C/180°C fan-forced.

3 Combine kumara, potato and salt in medium bowl; stand 5 minutes then squeeze out liquid.

4 Whisk egg in medium bowl; whisk in flour. Stir in onion and kumara mixture.

5 To make rösti, heat oil in large ovenproof frying pan over medium heat; add kumara mixture, press down firmly. Cook rösti about 3 minutes or until browned lightly. Transfer rösti to oven; bake, uncovered, about 20 minutes or until browned. Turn onto chopping board, cut rösti into eight wedges; serve with breakfast beans.

breakfast beans Heat oil in large saucepan, add onion and garlic; cook, stirring, until onion softens. Stir in undrained tomatoes, the water and beans; bring to the boil. Reduce heat; simmer, uncovered, about 10 minutes or until thick. Remove from heat; stir in parsley.

prep + cook time *35 minutes* serves *4*
nutritional count per serving *11.3g total fat (1.7g saturated fat); 1020kJ (244 cal); 25g carbohydrate; 7.8g protein; 5.6g fibre*

If your frying pan handle is not ovenproof, wrap it well in foil to protect it in the oven.

Cannellini beans are amazingly good for you. They are loaded with nutrients like iron, magnesium and folate, and are an excellent source of fibre.

PORRIDGE WITH BANANA AND BRAZIL NUTS

2 cups (500ml) water

1 cup (250ml) reduced-fat milk

1⅓ cups (120g) rolled oats

2 medium bananas (400g), sliced thickly

⅓ cup (55g) brazil nuts, sliced thinly

1 tablespoon honey

1⅓ cups (330ml) reduced-fat milk, extra

1 Combine the water and milk in medium saucepan; bring to the boil. Reduce heat; add oats. Simmer, stirring, about 5 minutes or until porridge is thick and creamy.

2 Serve porridge topped with banana, nuts, honey and extra milk.

prep + cook time *10 minutes* serves 4
nutritional count per serving *14.2g total fat (4.4g saturated fat); 1517kJ (363 cal); 44.9g carbohydrate; 12.3g protein; 5.5g fibre*

BARLEY WITH MIXED BERRIES

2¼ cups (560ml) water

1½ cups (375ml) reduced-fat milk

1 cup (200g) barley

½ teaspoon ground cinnamon

1 tablespoon golden syrup

⅓ cup (95g) low-fat yogurt

125g strawberries, halved

½ cup (75g) blueberries

½ cup (75g) raspberries

1 Combine the water, milk and barley in medium saucepan; bring to the boil, stirring. Reduce heat; simmer about 35 minutes or until liquid has evaporated and barley is tender.

2 Stir in cinnamon and golden syrup. Serve topped with yogurt and berries.

prep + cook time *45 minutes* serves 4
nutritional count per serving *2.7g total fat (1.1g saturated fat); 1116kJ (267 cal); 46.2g carbohydrate; 10.4g protein; 7.5g fibre*

FOOD FOR A SLIM BODY

BEEF AND VEGETABLE SOUP

cooking-oil spray

500g lean diced beef

1 medium brown onion (150g), chopped coarsely

1 clove garlic, crushed

¼ cup (70g) tomato paste

1.5 litre (6 cups) water

2 bay leaves

2 medium carrots (240g), chopped coarsely

2 stalks celery (300g), trimmed, chopped coarsely

¼ small cauliflower (250g), cut into florets

1 large zucchini (150g), chopped coarsely

½ cup (60g) frozen peas

½ cup coarsely chopped fresh flat-leaf parsley

1 Lightly spray heated large saucepan with oil. Cook beef, in batches, until browned; remove from pan.

2 Cook onion and garlic in same pan, stirring, until onion softens. Add paste; cook, stirring, 2 minutes.

3 Return beef to pan with the water and bay leaves; bring to the boil. Reduce heat; simmer, covered, 1 hour. Uncover; simmer about 30 minutes or until beef is tender.

4 Add carrot, celery, cauliflower and zucchini; simmer, uncovered, about 20 minutes or until vegetables are tender. Add peas; stir until hot.

5 Serve soup sprinkled with parsley.

prep + cook time *2 hours* serves 4
nutritional count per serving *4.9g total fat
(1.5g saturated fat); 1074kJ (257 cal);
10g carbohydrate; 39.2g protein; 6.4g fibre*

To gain and retain a slim body, eat vegetables, fruit, wholegrain foods and pulses, fish, lean meat, dairy products and eggs. No junk food.

LEEK, BEAN AND MUSHROOM BAKE

1 cup (200g) dried white beans

2 teaspoons olive oil

2 medium leeks (700g), sliced thinly

3 cloves garlic, crushed

350g swiss brown mushrooms, halved

2 stalks celery (300g), trimmed, chopped coarsely

½ cup (125ml) dry red wine

1 cup (250ml) vegetable stock

700g bottled tomato pasta sauce

3 sprigs fresh thyme

1 cup (120g) frozen peas

3 slices multigrain bread, toasted, halved

1 Place beans in medium bowl, cover with water. Stand overnight, drain; rinse under cold water, drain. Cook beans in medium saucepan of boiling water about 20 minutes or until tender; drain.

2 Preheat oven to 200°C/180°C fan-forced.

3 Heat oil in large flameproof dish; cook leek, garlic, mushrooms and celery, stirring, until vegetables soften. Add wine; bring to the boil. Boil, uncovered, until liquid is reduced by half. Add beans, stock, sauce and thyme; bring to the boil.

4 Cover dish, transfer to oven; bake 30 minutes. Stir in peas; bake, uncovered, about 20 minutes or until sauce thickens slightly. Serve bake with toast. Sprinkle with extra thyme.

prep + cook time *1 hour 20 minutes (+ standing)*
serves 6

nutritional count per serving *3.7g total fat (0.5g saturated fat); 949kJ (227 cal); 28.6g carbohydrate; 11.4g protein; 11g fibre*

We used dried cannellini beans in this recipe.

WARM CHICKEN AND LENTIL SALAD

1 cup (200g) australian green lentils

300g chicken breast fillets, sliced thinly

2 teaspoons finely grated lemon rind

1 clove garlic, crushed

2 tablespoons finely chopped fresh oregano

cooking-oil spray

1 medium red capsicum (200g), sliced thickly

1 medium zucchini (120g), sliced thinly

2 flat mushrooms (160g), sliced thinly

⅓ cup (80ml) lemon juice

80g baby spinach leaves

1 Cook lentils in medium saucepan of boiling water about 20 minutes or until tender; drain.
2 Meanwhile, combine chicken, rind, garlic and half the oregano in small bowl.
3 Lightly spray heated large frying pan with oil. Cook chicken, stirring, until cooked through. Remove chicken from pan; cover.
4 Cook vegetables in same pan with 1 tablespoon of the juice, stirring, until vegetables soften.
5 Combine lentils, chicken, vegetables and spinach with remaining oregano and juice in large bowl.
prep + cook time *40 minutes* serves *4*
nutritional count per serving *3.1g total fat (0.6g saturated fat); 1099kJ (263 cal); 22.5g carbohydrate; 32g protein; 9.6g fibre*

Two 400g cans rinsed, drained brown lentils can be used instead of the green lentils. Add them to the salad in step 5.

food for a slim body

19

SPICED LAMB CUTLETS WITH TOMATO AND PARSLEY SALAD

2 teaspoons ground cumin

2 teaspoons ground coriander

12 french-trimmed lamb cutlets (600g)

4 medium egg tomatoes (300g), quartered

1 lebanese cucumber (130g), chopped coarsely

½ cup (100g) reduced-fat cottage cheese

1 cup loosely packed fresh flat-leaf parsley leaves

2 teaspoons olive oil

2 tablespoons red wine vinegar

1 clove garlic, crushed

1 Combine spices and lamb in medium bowl.

2 Cook lamb and tomato, in batches, on heated oiled grill plate (or grill or barbecue).

3 Combine tomato with remaining ingredients in medium bowl to make salad.

4 Serve lamb with tomato and parsley salad.

prep + cook time *25 minutes* serves 4
nutritional count per serving *9.6g total fat (3.2g saturated fat); 807kJ (193 cal); 2.5g carbohydrate; 22.7g protein; 2g fibre*

SALMON, ORANGE AND FENNEL SALAD

2 medium oranges (480g)

400g sashimi salmon, sliced thinly (*see glossary*)

2 tablespoons white wine vinegar

2 baby fennel bulbs (260g)

1 stalk celery (150g), trimmed

3 cups (350g) firmly packed watercress sprigs

1 Segment oranges over small bowl; reserve ¼ cup juice.

2 Combine salmon, 1 tablespoon reserved juice and half the vinegar in medium bowl. Cover; refrigerate 10 minutes.

3 Meanwhile, using mandolin or V-slicer, slice fennel and celery thinly. Chop 1 tablespoon fennel tips; reserve.

4 Combine salmon mixture, orange segments, fennel, celery, fennel tips, watercress, remaining juice and remaining vinegar in large bowl.

prep time *30 minutes* serves 4

nutritional count per serving *7.5g total fat (1.6g saturated fat); 882kJ (211 cal); 9.1g carbohydrate; 23g protein; 6g fibre*

BARBECUED CHILLI PRAWN AND NOODLE SALAD

100g bean thread noodles

1kg uncooked medium king prawns

1 teaspoon finely grated lime rind

1 clove garlic, crushed

2cm piece fresh ginger (10g), grated

2 tablespoons sweet chilli sauce

2 tablespoons lime juice

1 tablespoon fish sauce

1 small red capsicum (150g), sliced thinly

1 medium carrot (120g), cut into matchsticks

1 small red onion (100g), sliced thinly

150g snow peas, trimmed, sliced thinly

1 cup firmly packed fresh coriander leaves

1 Place noodles in medium heatproof bowl, cover with boiling water; stand until tender, drain.

2 Meanwhile, shell and devein prawns, leaving tails intact. Combine prawns, rind, garlic, ginger and half the sweet chilli sauce in medium bowl. Cook prawns on heated oiled grill plate (or grill or barbecue) until changed in colour.

3 Combine prawns, noodles, remaining sweet chilli sauce, juice, fish sauce, vegetables and coriander in large bowl.

prep + cook time *35 minutes* serves 4
nutritional count per serving *5.9g total fat (2.6g saturated fat); 1145kJ (274 cal); 21.4g carbohydrate; 30.6g protein; 5g fibre*

OCEAN TROUT, WITH THREE BEAN SALAD AND BUTTERMILK DRESSING

400g ocean trout fillets

2 teaspoons finely grated lime rind

2 cloves garlic, crushed

400g baby new potatoes, quartered

200g green beans, trimmed, halved

200g yellow beans, trimmed, halved

300g frozen broad beans, thawed, peeled

1 cup (120g) frozen peas

buttermilk dressing

⅓ cup (80ml) buttermilk

2 tablespoons lime juice

1 tablespoon finely chopped fresh mint

1 Make buttermilk dressing.

2 Preheat oven to 200°C/180°C fan-forced. Line oiled oven tray with baking paper.

3 Rub fish all over with combined rind and garlic; place on tray. Roast fish about 15 minutes. Cool; flake fish.

4 Meanwhile, boil, steam or microwave potatoes until tender. Place green and yellow beans in medium saucepan of boiling water; simmer until tender. Add broad beans and peas for last 2 minutes of bean cooking time; drain, cool 5 minutes.

5 Combine fish with vegetables and dressing in large bowl.

buttermilk dressing Combine ingredients in screw-top jar; shake well.

prep + cook time *35 minutes* **serves** 4
nutritional count per serving *8.3g total fat (1.9g saturated fat); 1267kJ (303 cal); 20.1g carbohydrate; 30.7g protein; 11.1g fibre*

CHICKEN AND CORN SOUP

food for a slim body

cooking-oil spray

2 trimmed corn cobs (500g), kernels removed

4cm piece fresh ginger (20g), grated

2 cloves garlic, crushed

4 green onions, sliced thinly

4 cups (1 litre) water

4 cups (1 litre) chicken stock

200g chicken breast fillet

1 teaspoon light soy sauce

1 egg white, beaten lightly

1 Lightly spray heated large saucepan with oil. Cook corn, ginger, garlic and half the onion, stirring, until fragrant. Add the water and stock; bring to the boil.

2 Add chicken; reduce heat. Simmer, covered, about 10 minutes or until chicken is cooked. Cool chicken in broth 10 minutes. Remove chicken; shred meat finely.

3 Return broth to the boil; add chicken and sauce. Reduce heat; gradually stir in egg white.

4 Serve soup sprinkled with remaining onion.

prep + cook time *40 minutes* serves 4
nutritional count per serving *3.2g total fat (0.9g saturated fat); 769kJ (184 cal); 17.4g carbohydrate; 18.9g protein; 4.6g fibre*

STIR-FRIED SPICY SQUID AND OCTOPUS

500g squid hoods

2 teaspoons vegetable oil

500g baby octopus, chopped coarsely

1 fresh long red chilli, sliced thinly

2 cloves garlic, crushed

4 green onions, sliced thinly

1 medium yellow capsicum (200g), sliced thinly

2 tablespoons kecap manis

2 tablespoons fish sauce

¼ cup (60ml) chinese cooking wine

150g sugar snap peas, trimmed

1 cup (80g) bean sprouts, trimmed

1 Cut squid down centre to open out flat; score inside diagonally then slice thickly.
2 Heat half the oil in wok; stir-fry squid and octopus, in batches, until cooked. Remove from pan.
3 Heat remaining oil in wok; stir-fry chilli, garlic and half the onion until fragrant. Add capsicum; stir-fry until capsicum is tender.
4 Return seafood to wok with sauces, cooking wine, peas and sprouts; stir-fry until hot.
5 Serve stir-fry sprinkled with remaining onion.
prep + cook time *40 minutes* serves 4
nutritional count per serving *5.4g total fat (1.1g saturated fat); 1087kJ (260 cal); 5.7g carbohydrate; 43.4g protein; 2.5g fibre*

food for a slim body

GINGER PRAWN AND SUSHI RICE SALAD

¾ cup (150g) white short-grain rice

¾ cup (180ml) water

¼ cup (60ml) rice vinegar

2 teaspoons light soy sauce

4cm piece fresh ginger (20g), grated

1kg uncooked medium king prawns

1 clove garlic, crushed

cooking-oil spray

2 green onions, sliced thinly

1 lebanese cucumber (130g), peeled, seeded, sliced thinly

1 sheet toasted nori (yaki-nori), shredded finely

1 Rinse rice under cold water; drain. Place rice and the water in small saucepan; bring to the boil. Reduce heat; simmer, covered tightly, about 10 minutes or until water is absorbed and rice is tender. Transfer rice to large bowl; add vinegar, sauce and half the ginger, mix through gently.
2 Meanwhile, shell and devein prawns leaving tails intact. Combine prawns, garlic and remaining ginger in medium bowl. Lightly spray heated large frying pan with oil; cook prawn mixture, stirring, until prawns are changed in colour. Add prawns, onion and cucumber to rice mixture; sprinkle with nori.

prep + cook time *35 minutes (+ standing)*
serves *4*
nutritional count per serving *1.5g total fat (0.4g saturated fat); 1074kJ (257 cal); 30.6g carbohydrate; 28.5g protein; 1g fibre*

You can use sushi rice, if you prefer. It is available from most major supermarkets and Asian food shops. Toasted nori is also available from most supermarkets and Asian food stores. Use scissors to shred the nori.

Prawns have a sweet, delicate flavour and are packed full of protein. They are also very low in fat, making them a healthy and tasty meal choice.

MEDITERRANEAN WHITE FISH WITH BEANS AND OLIVES

cooking-oil spray

800g firm white fish fillets, skin on

250g cherry tomatoes, halved

420g can four-bean mix, rinsed, drained

¼ cup (60ml) lemon juice

¼ cup (60ml) vegetable stock

½ cup (60g) seeded black olives, chopped coarsely

½ cup coarsely chopped fresh flat-leaf parsley

1 Lightly spray heated large frying pan with oil. Cook fish, skin-side down, about 7 minutes or until skin is crisp. Remove fish from pan; cover.
2 Cook tomato in same pan until softened. Add beans, juice and stock; bring to the boil. Add olives; cook, stirring, until hot. Stir in parsley.
3 Serve fish with bean mixture.

prep + cook time *25 minutes* serves 4
nutritional count per serving *5.5g total fat (1.6g saturated fat); 1279kJ (306 cal); 14.9g carbohydrate; 45.9g protein; 5.7g fibre*

We used blue-eye fillets in this recipe.

food for a slim body

28

LEMON AND FENNEL SNAPPER

3 baby fennel bulbs (390g)

cooking-oil spray

4 whole baby snapper (1.4kg)

2 teaspoons finely grated lemon rind

1 medium lemon (140g), sliced thinly

¼ cup (60ml) lemon juice

1 Preheat oven to 220°C/200°C fan-forced.
2 Quarter fennel lengthways; chop and reserve 1 tablespoon fennel tips.
3 Lightly spray heated large shallow baking dish with oil; cook fennel over heat until browned lightly. Transfer to oven; roast fennel, uncovered, 15 minutes.
4 Meanwhile, score fish three times each side. Rub fish all over with rind; fill fish cavity with lemon slices. Roast fish on top of fennel, uncovered, about 20 minutes or until fish is cooked.
5 Serve fish and fennel sprinkled with juice and reserved tips.

prep + cook time *40 minutes* serves 4
nutritional count per serving *3.6g total fat (1.2g saturated fat); 861kJ (206 cal); 2.6g carbohydrate; 38.4g protein; 1.5g fibre*

food for a slim body

29

FOOD FOR GREAT SKIN AND HAIR

WHITE BEAN, GRAPEFRUIT AND HERB SALAD

2 ruby red grapefruits (700g)

2 teaspoons olive oil

1 tablespoon white wine vinegar

420g can butter beans, rinsed, drained

8 fresh dates (160g), seeded, chopped coarsely

50g baby spinach leaves

1 cup firmly packed fresh mint leaves

1 cup firmly packed fresh coriander leaves

1 Segment grapefruits over small bowl; reserve ¼ cup juice.

2 Whisk reserved juice with oil and vinegar in large bowl. Season to taste.

3 Add grapefruit and remaining ingredients to dressing in bowl; toss gently.

prep time *20 minutes* serves *4*

nutritional count per serving *2.9g total fat (0.4g saturated fat); 552kJ (132 cal); 20.0g carbohydrate; 3.7g protein; 5.1g fibre*

We used butter beans for this recipe, but you can use any white beans.

For clear, glowing skin and healthy, shiny hair, eat fresh fruit and vegies in season. That way nature will provide the correct balance of vitamins, minerals and antioxidants to correspond with each season's demands on your health.

GREEN GRAPE AND APPLE SPRITZER

Using an electric juicer, extract juice from 500g seedless green grapes and 1 coarsely chopped large apple. Combine with 2 cups chilled soda water and 1 thinly sliced lime in large jug.
prep time *10 minutes* serves *4*
nutritional count per serving *0.2g total fat (0g saturated fat); 410kJ (98 cal); 22.3g carbohydrate; 0.9g protein; 2.3g fibre*

FRESH VEGETABLE JUICE

Using an electric juicer, extract juice from 2 coarsely chopped large carrots, 2 coarsely chopped small tomatoes, 2 coarsely chopped trimmed celery stalks and 50g baby spinach leaves.
prep time *10 minutes* serves *2*
nutritional count per serving *0.4g total fat (0g saturated fat); 347kJ (83 cal); 11.4g carbohydrate; 3.4g protein; 7.8g fibre*

PEACH, PAPAYA AND RASPBERRY JUICE

Blend or process 1 coarsely chopped medium peach, 50g peeled and seeded, coarsely chopped red papaya, 50g raspberries and ¼ cup water until smooth.

prep time *10 minutes* serves *1*
nutritional count per serving *0.4g total fat (0g saturated fat); 351kJ (84 cal); 14.6g carbohydrate; 1.9g protein; 5.6g fibre*

APPLE, CRANBERRY AND PEAR JUICE

Using an electric juicer, extract juice from 2 coarsely chopped small apples, 2 coarsely chopped small pears and 1 cup thawed, frozen cranberries.

prep time *10 minutes* serves *2*
nutritional count per serving *0.3g total fat (0g saturated fat); 660kJ (158 cal); 34.2g carbohydrate; 2.1g protein; 7.5g fibre*

food for great skin and hair

GREEN GAZPACHO

2 lebanese cucumbers (260g), chopped coarsely

3 medium green capsicums (600g), chopped coarsely

2 stalks celery (300g), trimmed, chopped coarsely

1 medium red onion (170g), chopped coarsely

1 clove garlic, quartered

⅓ cup (50g) roasted pine nuts

½ cup firmly packed fresh coriander leaves

2 teaspoons finely grated lime rind

2 tablespoons lime juice

avocado salsa

1 small avocado (200g), chopped finely

2 green onions, sliced thinly

1 tablespoon finely chopped fresh coriander leaves

1 tablespoon lime juice

1 Blend or process ingredients until smooth; push through fine sieve into large jug; discard solids. Season to taste. Cover; refrigerate 3 hours.
2 Make avocado salsa close to serving time.
3 Serve bowls of gazpacho sprinkled with salsa.
avocado salsa Combine ingredients in small bowl.
prep time *25 minutes (+ refrigeration)* serves 6
nutritional count per serving *11g total fat (1.5g saturated fat); 589kJ (141 cal); 5.4g carbohydrate; 3.6g protein; 3.3g fibre*

food for great skin and hair

VEGETABLE PAELLA

1 tablespoon olive oil

1 small red onion (100g), chopped finely

1 medium red capsicum (200g), chopped finely

1 medium yellow capsicum (200g), chopped finely

1 teaspoon smoked paprika

200g swiss brown mushrooms, halved

1⅔ cups (330g) brown short-grain rice

pinch saffron threads

4 medium tomatoes (600g), chopped coarsely

1 litre (4 cups) vegetable stock

200g green beans, trimmed, chopped coarsely

1 cup (120g) frozen peas

2 tablespoons coarsely chopped fresh
flat-leaf parsley

1 lemon (140g), cut into wedges

1 Heat oil in large deep frying pan; cook onion and capsicums, stirring, until onion softens. Add paprika and mushrooms; cook, stirring, until mushrooms are tender. Add rice and saffron; stir to coat rice in vegetable mixture.
2 Add tomatoes and 1 cup of the stock; cook, stirring, until liquid is absorbed. Add remaining stock; cook, covered, stirring occasionally, about 1 hour or until liquid is absorbed and rice is tender.
3 Sprinkle beans and peas over rice. Cook, covered, about 10 minutes or until beans are tender. Season to taste.
4 Cover paella; stand 5 minutes. Sprinkle paella with parsley; serve with lemon wedges.
prep + cook time *1 hour 40 minutes* serves 6
nutritional count per serving *5.5g total fat (1g saturated fat); 1333kJ (319 cal); 51.2g carbohydrate; 11.4g protein; 7.4g fibre*

food for great skin and hair

TAMARI, LIME AND SESAME VEGETABLES

1 tablespoon vegetable oil

1 fresh long red chilli, sliced thinly

2cm piece fresh ginger (10g), grated

1 clove garlic, crushed

1 medium carrot (120g), halved lengthways, sliced thinly

1 medium red capsicum (200g), sliced thinly

100g fresh shiitake mushrooms, sliced thinly

115g baby corn, halved lengthways

400g gai lan, cut into 5cm lengths, leaves separated

¼ cup (60ml) water

100g enoki mushrooms, trimmed

150g snow peas, trimmed, halved

½ cup (125ml) vegetable stock

2 tablespoons tamari

1 tablespoon lime juice

1 teaspoon sesame oil

1 teaspoon toasted sesame seeds

1 medium lime, cut into wedges

1 Heat vegetable oil in wok; stir-fry chilli, ginger, garlic, carrot, capsicum, shiitake mushrooms, corn and gai lan stems with the water, until vegetables are tender.

2 Add gai lan leaves, enoki mushrooms, snow peas, stock, tamari, juice and sesame oil; stir-fry until hot. Season to taste.

3 Sprinkle with seeds; serve with lime wedges.

prep + cook time *30 minutes* serves *4*
nutritional count per serving 7.4g total fat (0.9g saturated fat); 723kJ (173 cal); 12.5g carbohydrate; 9g protein; 9.4g fibre

Tamari is a thick, dark sauce made mainly from soya beans but without the wheat used in standard soy sauce. It has a distinctively mellow flavour.

Sesame seeds are exceptionally high in iron, calcium and magnesium, and have strong antioxidant properties. They are great toasted and sprinkled on this dish, or any vegie dish.

PEACH, WATERCRESS AND SPICED WALNUT SALAD

¾ cup (75g) walnut pieces

1 egg white, beaten lightly

1 teaspoon sweet paprika

1 teaspoon ground cumin

1 teaspoon ground coriander

1 teaspoon ground cinnamon

3 cups (350g) firmly packed, trimmed watercress

2 medium peaches (300g), peeled, sliced thickly

1 small red onion (100g), sliced thinly

1 lebanese cucumber (130g), seeded, sliced thinly

lime yogurt dressing

⅓ cup (95g) low-fat yogurt

1 teaspoon finely grated lime rind

1 tablespoon lime juice

1 Preheat oven to 200°C/180°C fan-forced. Line greased oven tray with baking paper.
2 Combine nuts with egg white in small bowl; drain nuts, toss in combined spices. Place nuts, in single layer, on oven tray; roast about 5 minutes or until crisp. Cool.
3 Meanwhile, make lime yogurt dressing.
4 Combine nuts with remaining ingredients and dressing in large bowl. Season to taste.
lime yogurt dressing Whisk ingredients in small bowl until combined.

prep + cook time *25 minutes* serves *4*
nutritional count per serving *13.3g total fat (0.8g saturated fat); 794kJ (190 cal); 7.7g carbohydrate; 7.4g protein; 4.4g fibre*

BALSAMIC ROASTED RATATOUILLE WITH CHICKPEAS

1 tablespoon olive oil

1 large red onion (300g), sliced thickly

3 cloves garlic, crushed

2 tablespoons balsamic vinegar

400g pumpkin, cut into 2cm pieces

1 medium red capsicum (200g), cut into 2cm pieces

2 medium zucchini (240g), sliced thickly

1 medium eggplant (300g), cut into 2cm pieces

150g button mushrooms

2 x 410g cans crushed tomatoes

400g can chickpeas, rinsed, drained

¼ cup finely chopped fresh flat-leaf parsley

1 teaspoon finely grated lemon rind

1 Preheat oven to 220°C/200°C fan-forced.
2 Heat oil in large baking dish; cook onion and garlic, stirring, until onion is soft. Add vinegar, pumpkin, capsicum, zucchini, eggplant and mushrooms; transfer to oven. Roast, uncovered, about 40 minutes or until vegetables are tender.
3 Add undrained tomatoes and chickpeas; roast, uncovered, 10 minutes. Season to taste.
4 Serve ratatouille sprinkled with parsley and rind.
prep + cook time *1 hour* serves 4
nutritional count per serving *7.3g total fat (1.1g saturated fat); 1070kJ (256 cal); 29.3g carbohydrate; 11.9g protein; 12.1g fibre*

food for great skin and hair

CRANBERRY MACERATED BERRIES

250g strawberries, quartered

125g raspberries

125g blueberries

1 tablespoon pure icing sugar

½ cup (125ml) apple, cranberry and
   pomegranate juice

2 teaspoons finely grated orange rind

½ cup (140g) low-fat vanilla-flavoured yogurt

1 Combine berries, icing sugar, juice and rind in medium bowl. Cover, refrigerate 3 hours.
2 Serve berry mixture with yogurt.
prep time *10 minutes (+ refrigeration)* serves 4
nutritional count per serving *0.3g total fat (0.1g saturated fat); 422kJ (101 cal); 18.1g carbohydrate; 3.7g protein; 3.9g fibre*

TROPICAL SALAD WITH LIME GINGER SYRUP

565g can lychees, drained, halved

2 medium kiwifruit (170g), halved lengthways, sliced thickly

2 medium gold kiwifruit (170g), halved lengthways, sliced thickly

½ small pineapple (450g), peeled, sliced thickly

60g fresh coconut, grated coarsely

2 tablespoons finely shredded fresh mint

lime and ginger syrup

½ cup (125ml) water

2 tablespoons grated palm sugar

1 tablespoon lime juice

2cm piece fresh ginger (10g), sliced thinly

1 teaspoon finely grated lime rind

1 Make lime and ginger syrup.
2 Combine fruit and coconut in large bowl with syrup; cover, refrigerate 1 hour. Serve sprinkled with mint.

lime and ginger syrup Combine the water, sugar, juice and ginger in small saucepan; stir over heat until sugar dissolves, bring to the boil. Boil, uncovered, about 5 minutes or until syrup thickens. Remove from heat; stir in rind. Cool.

*prep + cook time 25 minutes
(+ cooking and refrigeration) serves 4
nutritional count per serving 4.5g total fat
(3.6g saturated fat); 932kJ (223 cal);
40.2g carbohydrate; 2.9g protein; 6.6g fibre*

You need the flesh from about half a coconut. To crack the coconut, pierce one of the eyes, put it into a preheated oven 240°C/220°C fan-forced for about 15 minutes.

food for great skin and hair

41

FOOD FOR ENERGY AND STAMINA

WASABI, SOY AND SESAME NOODLES

180g dried soba noodles

2 teaspoons vegetable oil

400g gai lan, cut into 3cm lengths, leaves separated

175g broccolini, cut into 3cm lengths

150g snow peas, trimmed

1 tablespoon light soy sauce

2 tablespoons rice wine vinegar

¼ cup (60ml) vegetable stock

2 teaspoons wasabi

2 teaspoons toasted sesame seeds

1 Cook noodles in medium saucepan of boiling water until tender; drain.

2 Heat oil in wok; stir-fry gai lan stems and broccolini until tender. Add noodles, gai lan leaves, snow peas, sauce, vinegar, stock and wasabi; stir-fry until hot. Season to taste.

3 Serve stir-fry sprinkled with seeds.

prep + cook time *25 minutes* serves 4
nutritional count per serving *4.4g total fat (0.7g saturated fat); 1016kJ (243 cal); 34.5g carbohydrate; 11.5g protein; 8.1g fibre*

Carbohydrates give you energy and stamina. The trick is to work out how much you need – if you don't use the carbs by expending energy, you'll gain weight. Eat dried (or canned) beans, peas and lentils, rice, pasta, noodles and wholegrain foods as part of a balanced diet.

ROASTED CAPSICUM, TOMATO AND BORLOTTI BEAN SALAD

1 cup (200g) dried borlotti beans

2 small red capsicums (300g), quartered, seeds and membranes removed

3 medium egg tomatoes (225g), quartered

60g baby rocket leaves

balsamic and oregano dressing

1 tablespoon olive oil

1 tablespoon balsamic vinegar

2 teaspoons finely chopped fresh oregano

1 clove garlic, crushed

1 Place beans in medium bowl, cover with water; stand overnight, drain. Cook beans in medium saucepan of boiling water about 30 minutes or until tender; rinse under cold water, drain.

2 Preheat oven to 200°C/180°C fan-forced. Line two oiled oven trays with baking paper.

3 Place capsicum, skin-side up, on trays with tomato. Roast, uncovered, about 35 minutes or until skin blisters and blackens on capsicum and tomatoes soften. Cover capsicum with plastic wrap for 5 minutes; peel then slice thickly.

4 Make balsamic and oregano dressing.

5 Combine beans, capsicum, tomato, rocket and dressing in large bowl; season to taste.

balsamic and oregano dressing Combine ingredients in screw-top jar; shake well. Season to taste.

prep + cook time *55 minutes (+ standing)*
serves *4*
nutritional count per serving *5.2g total fat (0.7g saturated fat); 598kJ (143 cal); 17.1g carbohydrate; 6.4g protein; 3.5g fibre*

BROAD BEAN PATTIES WITH MINTED YOGURT

500g frozen broad beans

½ cup (100g) green split peas

1 medium brown onion (150g), chopped finely

2 cloves garlic, crushed

⅓ cup (50g) wholemeal plain flour

¼ cup (25g) packaged breadcrumbs

1 egg

cooking-oil spray

minted yogurt

⅔ cup (190g) low-fat yogurt

1 teaspoon finely grated lime rind

2 tablespoons lime juice

¼ cup finely chopped fresh mint

1 Place beans in medium saucepan of boiling water, return to the boil; drain. When beans are cool enough to handle, peel.
2 Place peas in medium saucepan of boiling water; reduce heat. Simmer until tender, drain. Mash beans and peas together in large bowl; cool.
3 Mix onion, garlic, flour, breadcrumbs and egg into bean mixture; season to taste. Using wet hands, shape mixture into eight patties; place on baking-paper-lined tray. Cover; refrigerate 30 minutes.
4 Meanwhile, make minted yogurt.
5 Lightly spray heated large frying pan with oil; cook patties, in batches, until browned lightly and heated through.
6 Serve patties with minted yogurt.
minted yogurt Whisk ingredients in small bowl until combined; season to taste.
prep + cook time *40 minutes (+ refrigeration)*
serves *4*
nutritional count per serving *3.6g total fat (0.7g saturated fat); 1087kJ (260 cal); 30.7g carbohydrate; 19.8g protein; 11.5g fibre*

food for energy and stamina

WHOLEMEAL BEETROOT AND GOAT'S CHEESE PIZZAS

¼ cup (45g) cracked buckwheat

½ cup (125ml) warm water

½ teaspoon caster sugar

1 teaspoon dried yeast

¾ cup (110g) plain flour

¾ cup (120g) wholemeal plain flour

2 large beetroot (400g)

8 shallots (200g), peeled

½ cup (140g) tomato paste

120g goat's cheese

40g baby rocket leaves

1 Place buckwheat in small heatproof bowl; cover with boiling water. Stand 30 minutes, covered. Rinse under cold water; drain.

2 Combine the water, sugar and yeast in small jug, cover; stand in warm place about 10 minutes or until frothy.

3 Combine buckwheat and sifted flours in large bowl. Add yeast mixture; mix to a soft dough. Knead dough on floured surface about 10 minutes or until smooth and elastic. Place dough in oiled large bowl. Cover; stand in warm place about 45 minutes or until doubled in size.

4 Meanwhile, preheat oven to 220°C/200°C fan-forced. Oil two large oven trays.

5 Trim leaves from beetroot, wrap unpeeled beetroot in foil; place in small shallow baking dish. Roast beetroot 20 minutes. Add shallots to dish; roast about 30 minutes or until vegetables are tender. Cool 10 minutes. Peel beetroot; chop coarsely. Cut shallots into small wedges.

6 Divide dough into four. Roll each piece into 15cm rounds; place on trays.

7 Bake bases 10 minutes. Remove from oven; spread bases with paste, sprinkle with cheese. Bake bases about 8 minutes or until crisp.

8 Top pizzas with beetroot, shallots and rocket. Season to taste.

prep + cook time *45 minutes (+ standing)*
makes *4*
nutritional count per pizza *6.4g total fat (3.3g saturated fat); 1613kJ (386 cal); 61.3g carbohydrate; 15.6g protein; 9.5g fibre.*

Wear disposable gloves when handling the cooked beetroot. When you squeeze the warm beetroot, the skin will burst and peel away easily

EGGPLANT AND TABBOULEH STACKS WITH CHICKPEA PURÉE

¼ cup (40g) burghul

2 medium tomatoes (300g)

1 cup firmly packed fresh flat-leaf parsley leaves

1 large eggplant (500g)

cooking-oil spray

chickpea purée

125g can chickpeas, rinsed, drained

¼ cup (70g) yogurt

1 tablespoon tahini

½ teaspoon finely grated lemon rind

1 tablespoon lemon juice

1 clove garlic, quartered

1 Make chickpea purée.
2 To make tabbouleh, place burghul in small bowl. Seed tomatoes; reserve juice. Combine tomato seeds and juice with burghul; cover, stand 30 minutes. Chop tomato flesh finely. Combine tomato with burghul and parsley in medium bowl.
3 Peel alternate lengthwise strips of skin from eggplant; slice eggplant into thin rounds. Lightly spray eggplant with oil. Cook eggplant on heated oiled grill plate (or grill or barbecue) until tender.
4 Layer eggplant, tabbouleh and chickpea purée on serving plates.

chickpea purée Blend or process ingredients until smooth; season to taste.

prep + cook time *35 minutes (+ standing)* serves 4
nutritional count per serving *5g total fat (0.8g saturated fat); 619kJ (148 cal); 14.9g carbohydrate; 6.7g protein; 7.5g fibre*

food for energy and stamina

48

GRILLED VEGETABLE AND BLACK-EYE BEAN SALAD

1 cup (200g) dried black-eye beans

2 cloves garlic, unpeeled

2 flat mushrooms (160g), sliced thinly

2 medium zucchini (240g), sliced thinly lengthways

250g cherry tomatoes

1 tablespoon olive oil

1 teaspoon finely grated lemon rind

2 tablespoons lemon juice

1 teaspoon finely chopped fresh thyme

60g baby rocket leaves

1 Place beans in medium bowl, cover with water; stand overnight, drain. Cook beans in medium saucepan of boiling water about 20 minutes or until tender; drain. Rinse under cold water; drain.

2 Meanwhile, cook garlic, mushrooms, zucchini and tomatoes, in batches, on heated oiled grill plate (or grill or barbecue) until tender.

3 Peel garlic; crush. Whisk garlic, oil, rind, juice and thyme in large bowl.

4 Add beans, vegetables and rocket to bowl with garlic mixture; toss gently. Season to taste.

prep + cook time *1 hour (+ standing)* serves 4
nutritional count per serving *5.4g total fat 0.7g saturated fat); 568kJ (136 cal); 12.4g carbohydrate; 7.1g protein; 6.3g fibre*

food for energy and stamina

CAULIFLOWER, LENTIL AND PEA CURRY

cooking-oil spray

1 medium brown onion (150g), sliced thickly

1 clove garlic, crushed

2cm piece fresh ginger (10g), grated

1 fresh long red chilli, chopped finely

1 teaspoon ground cumin

½ teaspoon ground turmeric

¼ teaspoon ground cardamom

¼ teaspoon ground fennel

1 tablespoon tomato paste

1 small cauliflower (1kg), trimmed, chopped coarsely

2 cups (500ml) vegetable stock

400g can crushed tomatoes

270ml can light coconut cream

½ cup (100g) dried red lentils

1 cup (120g) frozen peas

½ cup firmly packed fresh coriander leaves

1 Lightly spray heated large saucepan with oil; cook onion, garlic, ginger and chilli, stirring, until onion softens. Add spices and paste; cook, stirring, about 2 minutes or until fragrant.

2 Add cauliflower, stock, undrained tomatoes, coconut cream and lentils; bring to the boil. Reduce heat; simmer, uncovered, about 10 minutes or until cauliflower and lentils are tender. Add peas; stir until hot. Season to taste.

3 Serve curry sprinkled with coriander.

prep + cook time *35 minutes* serves *4*
nutritional count per serving *12.7g total fat (9.5g saturated fat); 1267kJ (303 cal); 24.8g carbohydrate; 16.7g protein; 12.7g fibre*

This vegetarian curry is a delicious combination of spices and flavours, and built into all that pleasure is plenty of long-lasting energy and a steady supply of nutrients.

WHOLEMEAL VEGETABLE SPAGHETTI WITH GARLIC CRUMBS

6 slices wholemeal bread (270g), discard crusts

375g wholemeal spaghetti

200g broccoli, cut into small florets

150g sugar snap peas, trimmed

1 tablespoon olive oil

2 cloves garlic, crushed

1 medium zucchini (120g), sliced thinly

2 drained anchovy fillets, chopped finely

2 green onions, chopped finely

2 teaspoons finely grated lemon rind

¼ cup (60ml) lemon juice

1 Process bread until fine.
2 Cook pasta in large saucepan of boiling water until tender. Add broccoli and peas to water for last 5 minutes of pasta cooking time. Drain; reserve ¼ cup cooking liquid.
3 Meanwhile, heat half the oil in large frying pan; cook breadcrumbs and garlic until browned and crisp. Remove from pan.
4 Heat remaining oil in same cleaned pan; cook zucchini, anchovy and onion until zucchini is tender.
5 Combine pasta mixture and zucchini mixture in large bowl with rind, juice and reserved cooking liquid. Season to taste.
6 Serve pasta sprinkled with garlic crumbs.

prep + cook time *40 minutes* serves *4*
nutritional count per serving *9.1g total fat (1.2g saturated fat); 2299kJ (550 cal); 85.5g carbohydrate; 21.9g protein; 16.5g fibre*

BROWN RICE WITH ASPARAGUS, SPINACH AND ALMONDS

2 teaspoons olive oil

1 medium leek (350g), sliced thinly

1½ cups (300g) brown long-grain rice

1¼ cups (310ml) water

1 cup (250ml) chicken stock

170g asparagus, trimmed, cut into 3cm lengths

40g baby spinach leaves

¼ cup (35g) roasted slivered almonds

1 Heat oil in medium saucepan; cook leek, stirring, about 10 minutes or until leek softens. Add rice; stir to coat in leek mixture. Add the water and stock; bring to the boil. Reduce heat; simmer, covered tightly, about 35 minutes or until rice is tender.

2 Remove rice from heat; top with asparagus; stand, covered, 10 minutes.

3 Stir in spinach; season to taste. Serve rice sprinkled with nuts.

prep + cook time *55 minutes* serves *4*
nutritional count per serving *9.5g total fat (1.1g saturated fat); 1613kJ (386 cal); 61.6g carbohydrate; 10.6g protein; 5.7g fibre*

food for energy and stamina

BARLEY, PUMPKIN AND MUSHROOM RISOTTO

1 litre (4 cups) water

2 cups (500ml) salt-reduced chicken stock

2 tablespoons olive oil

300g pumpkin, cut into 1cm pieces

200g swiss brown mushrooms, sliced thinly

1 medium brown onion (150g), chopped finely

2 cloves garlic, crushed

¾ cup (150g) barley

½ cup (125ml) dry white wine

1 tablespoon coarsely chopped fresh sage

1 Combine the water and stock in medium saucepan; bring to the boil. Reduce heat; simmer, covered.

2 Heat half the oil in large saucepan; cook pumpkin, stirring, until tender. Add mushrooms; cook, stirring, until mushrooms are tender. Remove vegetables from pan.

3 Heat remaining oil in same pan; cook onion and garlic, stirring, until onion softens. Stir in barley. Add wine; bring to the boil. Reduce heat; simmer, stirring, until wine is absorbed.

4 Add ½ cup of the simmering stock mixture; cook, stirring, over low heat until liquid is absorbed. Continue adding stock mixture, in ½-cup batches, stirring until liquid is absorbed after each addition. Total cooking time should be about 50 minutes or until barley is tender.

5 Add vegetable mixture and sage to risotto; stir until hot. Season to taste.

prep + cook time *1 hour 20 minutes* serves 4
nutritional count per serving *11g total fat (1.9g saturated fat); 1208kJ (289 cal); 30.8g carbohydrate; 8.4g protein; 7g fibre*

Barley is rich in fibre and full of nutritious goodness. It has a lovely nutty flavour and chewy texture, making it a perfect low-GI alternative to a traditional rice risotto.

LOW-GI FRIED RICE WITH OMELETTE

1⅓ cups (265g) white long-grain rice

1½ cups (375ml) water

1 tablespoon peanut oil

3 eggs, beaten lightly

2 cloves garlic, crushed

3cm piece fresh ginger (15g), grated

1 fresh long red chilli, sliced thinly

1 small red capsicum (150g), cut into 1cm pieces

115g baby corn, cut into 1cm pieces

100g green beans, trimmed, cut into 1cm pieces

100g fresh shiitake mushrooms, sliced thinly

¼ cup (60ml) light soy sauce

2 tablespoons rice vinegar

½ cup (40g) bean sprouts, trimmed

4 green onions, sliced thinly

1 Place rice into medium saucepan; cover with the water, bring to the boil. Reduce heat; simmer, covered, about 15 minutes or until water is absorbed and rice is tender. Cool.
2 Heat half the oil in wok; pour in half the egg, tilt wok to coat with egg. Cook until omelette is set. Remove omelette; roll tightly. Repeat with remaining egg. Slice omelettes thinly.
3 Heat remaining oil in wok; stir-fry garlic, ginger and chilli until fragrant. Add vegetables; stir-fry until tender.
4 Add rice, sauce, vinegar and sprouts; stir-fry until hot. Season to taste. Stir in half the onions.
5 Serve rice topped with remaining onion and omelette strips.

prep + cook time 45 minutes (+ cooling) serves 4
nutritional count per serving 10g total fat (2.3g saturated fat); 1685kJ (403 cal); 60.6g carbohydrate; 14.7g protein; 4.3g fibre

Rice can be cooked the day before; store, covered, in the fridge.

CRISPY TOFU WITH SOY AND GINGER BUCKWHEAT SALAD

300g firm tofu, cut into 8 slices

¼ cup (45g) rice flour

cooking-oil spray

soy and ginger buckwheat salad

1 tablespoon peanut oil

1 tablespoon light soy sauce

1cm piece fresh ginger (5g), grated

2 tablespoons lime juice

2 teaspoons brown sugar

100g snow peas, sliced thinly

1 medium carrot (120g), cut into matchsticks

1 small red capsicum (150g), sliced thinly

1 cup (80g) bean sprouts, trimmed

⅓ cup (65g) roasted buckwheat kernels

½ cup coarsely chopped fresh coriander

1 Place tofu, in single layer, on tray lined with absorbent paper; cover with more absorbent paper, stand 10 minutes.

2 Make soy and ginger buckwheat salad.

3 Coat tofu in flour; shake off excess. Lightly spray heated large frying pan with oil; cook tofu, in batches, until browned.

4 Serve tofu with salad.

soy and ginger buckwheat salad Combine peanut oil, sauce, ginger, juice and sugar in large bowl; whisk well. Add remaining ingredients; toss gently. Season to taste.

prep + cook time *30 minutes* serves *4*
nutritional count per serving   *11.3g total fat (1.8g saturated fat); 117.9kJ (282 cal); 26.8g carbohydrate; 14g protein; 8.4g fibre*

If you can't find roasted buckwheat kernels, roast the kernels in the oven at 180°C/160°C fan-forced for about 5 minutes; cool before using.

food for energy and stamina

FOOD FOR STRONG BONES AND TEETH

CHILLI, CORIANDER, LAMB AND BARLEY SALAD

⅔ cup (130g) barley

1 tablespoon olive oil

1 teaspoon dried chilli flakes

1 tablespoon finely chopped fresh coriander

500g lamb back straps

250g baby egg tomatoes, quartered

100g baby spinach leaves

100g reduced-fat fetta cheese, crumbled

lemon dressing

2 tablespoons lemon juice

1 tablespoon olive oil

¼ teaspoon caster sugar

1 Cook barley in medium saucepan of boiling water, uncovered, about 25 minutes or until tender; drain. Cool 10 minutes.

2 Meanwhile, combine oil, chilli, coriander and lamb in medium bowl. Cook lamb on heated oiled grill plate (or grill or barbecue). Cover lamb; stand 5 minutes then slice thickly.

3 Make lemon dressing.

4 Combine lamb, barley, tomato and dressing. Serve with spinach and crumbled cheese.

lemon dressing Combine ingredients in screw-top jar; shake well.

prep + cook time *40 minutes* serves *4*

nutritional count per serving *20.9g total fat (6.2g saturated fat); 1822kJ (436 cal); 21.8g carbohydrate; 37.4g protein; 5.1g fibre*

Eat foods that are rich in calcium every day, not only to build and maintain strong bones and teeth, but also to help the body absorb vitamins. Dairy foods, soy products and green leafy vegetables are the main sources of calcium.

CELERY, SPINACH AND GRAPE JUICE

Using an electric juicer, extract juice from 1 coarsely chopped trimmed celery stalk, 1 cup seedless green grapes and 30g baby spinach leaves.

prep time *5 minutes* serves *1*
nutritional count per serving *0.4g total fat (0g saturated fat); 552kJ (132 cal); 28.6g carbohydrate; 2.4g protein; 4.2g fibre*

SILVER BEET AND APPLE JUICE

Using an electric juicer, extract juice from 1 coarsely chopped lebanese cucumber, 1 coarsely chopped large apple, 1 coarsely chopped silver beet leaf and 6 fresh mint leaves.

prep time *5 minutes* serves *1*
nutritional count per serving *0.4g total fat (0g saturated fat); 422kJ (101 cal); 20.2g carbohydrate; 1.9g protein; 5.5g fibre*

BANANA RASPBERRY SMOOTHIE

Blend or process ½ small sliced banana, ¼ cup raspberries, ¾ cup milk and 1 teaspoon honey until smooth.

prep time *5 minutes* serves *1*
nutritional count per serving *2.7g total fat (1.7g saturated fat); 305kJ (73 cal); 9.4g carbohydrate; 2.7g protein; 1.1g fibre*

SOY AND MANGO SMOOTHIE

Blend or process ½ coarsely chopped medium mango, ¾ cup soy milk, 1 teaspoon wheat germ and 1 teaspoon honey until smooth.

prep time *5 minutes* serves *1*
nutritional count per serving *5.5g total fat (0.6g saturated fat); 907kJ (217 cal); 33.7g carbohydrate; 7.9g protein; 3.3g fibre*

food for strong bones and teeth

TUNA KEBABS WITH SNOW PEA AND SPINACH SALAD

2 tablespoons sake

2 tablespoons mirin

2 teaspoons red miso paste

2 teaspoons brown sugar

2 teaspoons light soy sauce

4 x 150g tuna steaks, halved lengthways

snow pea and spinach salad

150g snow peas, halved diagonally

2 teaspoons rice vinegar

1 teaspoon light soy sauce

1 teaspoon peanut oil

pinch caster sugar

100g baby spinach leaves

1 tablespoon sesame seeds, toasted

1 Combine sake, mirin, paste, sugar and sauce in small jug. Thread fish onto eight bamboo skewers; place in single layer in large shallow dish. Pour sake mixture over skewers. Cover, refrigerate 2 hours.
2 Make snow pea and spinach salad.
3 Cook fish skewers on heated oiled grill plate (or grill or barbecue).
4 Serve skewers with salad.
snow pea and spinach salad Boil, steam or microwave snow peas until tender; rinse under cold water, drain. Whisk vinegar, sauce, oil and sugar in large bowl. Add snow peas, spinach and seeds; toss gently.

prep + cook time *35 minutes (+ refrigeration)*
serves *4*

nutritional count per serving *11.8g total fat (3.9g saturated fat); 1246kJ (298 cal); 4.4g carbohydrate; 40.6g protein; 2g fibre*

Soak bamboo skewers in water for at least 30 minutes to prevent burning during cooking.

food for strong bones and teeth

SOYA BEAN CASSEROLE

1 tablespoon olive oil

2 stalks celery (300g), trimmed, chopped coarsely

1 medium brown onion (150g), chopped coarsely

1 medium carrot (120g), chopped coarsely

2 cloves garlic, crushed

2 tablespoons tomato paste

400g can crushed tomatoes

½ cup (125ml) vegetable stock

½ cup (125ml) water

4 fresh thyme sprigs

2 x 400g cans soya beans, rinsed, drained

⅓ cup (25g) finely grated parmesan cheese

2 teaspoons fresh thyme leaves

1 Heat oil in large saucepan; cook celery, onion, carrot and garlic, stirring, until onion softens. Add paste; cook, stirring, 1 minute. Add undrained tomatoes, stock, the water and thyme sprigs; bring to the boil. Reduce heat, simmer, covered, 35 minutes.

2 Add beans; simmer, covered, 10 minutes. Serve casserole sprinkled with cheese and thyme leaves.

prep + cook time *1 hour 10 minutes* serves 4
nutritional count per serving *14.1g total fat (3g saturated fat); 1078kJ (258 cal); 11.2g carbohydrate; 16g protein; 10g fibre*

CHILLI TOFU STIR-FRY

300g firm silken tofu

1 tablespoon peanut oil

1 medium red onion (170g), sliced thinly

2 cloves garlic, crushed

1 fresh long red chilli, sliced thinly

1 large red capsicum (350g), chopped coarsely

350g broccolini, cut into 3cm lengths

300g gai lan, chopped coarsely

300g choy sum, chopped coarsely

¼ cup (60ml) hoisin sauce

¼ cup (60ml) oyster sauce

2 tablespoons water

1 lime, cut into wedges

1 Cut tofu into 2cm cubes; spread, in single layer, on tray lined with absorbent paper. Cover tofu with more absorbent paper; stand 10 minutes.
2 Heat half the oil in wok; stir-fry tofu, in batches, until browned lightly. Drain on absorbent paper.
3 Heat remaining oil in wok; stir-fry onion, garlic and chilli until onion softens. Add capsicum and broccolini; stir-fry until vegetables are tender. Add gai lan, choy sum, sauces and the water; stir-fry until gai lan wilts.
4 Return tofu to wok; stir-fry until combined. Serve with lime wedges.

prep + cook time *35 minutes* serves 4
nutritional count per serving *7.8g total fat (1.2g saturated fat); 1016kJ (243 cal); 18.7g carbohydrate; 17.4g protein; 13.4g fibre*

ZUCCHINI-FLOWER AND TOMATO FRITTATA

6 baby zucchini with flowers attached (120g)

150g reduced-fat ricotta cheese

8 eggs

¼ cup (60ml) milk

⅓ cup (50g) drained semi-dried tomatoes, chopped coarsely

100g reduced-fat fetta cheese, crumbled

1 Preheat oven to 220°C/200°C fan-forced.

2 Discard stamens from zucchini flowers; fill flowers with ricotta, twist petal tops to enclose filling.

3 Whisk eggs and milk in large jug. Pour egg mixture into heated oiled medium ovenproof frying pan. Top with zucchini flowers, tomatoes and fetta. Cook frittata, over medium heat, about 5 minutes or until bottom sets. Transfer to oven; bake, uncovered, about 15 minutes or until frittata is set. Slide onto serving plate; cut into wedges.

prep + cook time 35 minutes serves 4
nutritional count per serving 20.5g total fat (8.6g saturated fat); 1354kJ (324 cal); 6.6g carbohydrate; 27.6g protein; 2.3g fibre

You will need an ovenproof frying pan with a 17cm base for this recipe. If necessary, protect the handle of the pan by wrapping it in foil.

food for strong bones and teeth

SPINACH AND EGGPLANT LASAGNE STACKS

1 tablespoon olive oil

2 stalks celery (300g), trimmed, chopped finely

1 medium brown onion (150g), chopped finely

2 cloves garlic, crushed

500g beef mince

700ml bottled tomato pasta sauce

2 tablespoons tomato paste

¼ cup finely chopped fresh flat-leaf parsley

2 medium eggplants (600g)

50g baby spinach leaves

1 cup (120g) coarsely grated cheddar cheese

cheese sauce

40g butter

2 tablespoons plain flour

1½ cups (375ml) hot milk

½ cup (60g) coarsely grated cheddar cheese

1 Heat oil in large saucepan; cook celery, onion and garlic, stirring, until onion softens. Add mince; cook, stirring, until meat changes colour. Add sauce and paste; bring to the boil, stirring. Reduce heat, simmer, uncovered, about 20 minutes or until sauce thickens. Stir in parsley.

2 Meanwhile, make cheese sauce.

3 Thinly slice eggplant lengthways to give 18 slices. Cook, in batches, on heated oiled grill plate (or grill or barbecue) until browned lightly and tender.

4 Preheat grill.

5 Divide one third of the beef mixture between six heatproof plates, top each with one third of the spinach then one slice of eggplant; spoon over one third of the cheese sauce. Repeat to make three layers; sprinkle with cheese. Grill until cheese is melted and browned lightly.

cheese sauce Melt butter in medium saucepan. Add flour; cook, stirring, until mixture bubbles. Remove from heat; gradually stir in milk. Stir over medium heat until sauce boils and thickens. Remove sauce from heat; stir in cheese.

prep + cook time *1 hour 10 minutes* serves 6
nutritional count per serving *29.2g total fat (14.5g saturated fat); 1994kJ (477 cal); 20.1g carbohydrate; 31.1g protein; 7g fibre*

These delicious lasagne stacks use grilled eggplant slices instead of lasagne sheets, making it a lighter version of the usually heavy traditional lasagne.

CHEESY OMELETTES

4 eggs

2 tablespoons water

10g butter

⅓ cup (40g) coarsely grated cheddar cheese

1 Beat eggs and the water with fork in medium jug. Melt half the butter in medium frying pan; swirl pan to coat with butter. Pour half the egg mixture into pan; tilt pan to spread mixture evenly, cook over medium heat until almost set.

2 Sprinkle half the cheese over omelette; fold omelette in half. Slide omelette onto plate; keep warm. Repeat to make another omelette.

prep + cook time *15 minutes* makes *2*
nutritional count per omelette *22.8g total fat (10.7g saturated fat); 1191kJ (285 cal); 0.4g carbohydrate; 20.2g protein; 0g fibre*

You need a frying pan with a 20cm base.
Add finely chopped fresh parsley or chives
to the egg mixture before cooking.

food for strong bones and teeth

YOGURT AND MIXED BERRY POPS

2 tablespoons water

1 teaspoon powdered gelatine

1½ cups (225g) frozen mixed berries, thawed

2 cups (560g) low-fat vanilla yogurt

1 Place the water in small heatproof jug; sprinkle gelatine over water. Stand jug in small saucepan of simmering water; stir until gelatine dissolves.
2 Blend or process berries until smooth; strain through fine sieve into large jug, discard seeds.
3 Add yogurt and gelatine mixture to berry puree. Divide mixture evenly between eight (⅓-cup/80ml) ice-block moulds. Freeze 3 hours or overnight.
prep + cook time *20 minutes (+ freezing)*
makes *8*
nutritional count per pop *0.2g total fat (0.1g saturated fat); 268kJ (64 cal); 9.4g carbohydrate; 5.1g protein; 0.6g fibre*

food for strong bones and teeth

DETOXING FOOD

UDON NOODLE SALAD WITH BUK CHOY AND SHIITAKE

270g dried udon noodles

1 cup dried shiitake mushrooms (25g)

400g buk choy, shredded coarsely

5cm piece fresh ginger (25g), cut into matchsticks

2 teaspoons black sesame seeds

mirin and tamari dressing

1 tablespoon mirin

1 tablespoon rice wine vinegar

2 tablespoons tamari

1 clove garlic, crushed

1 Make mirin and tamari dressing.
2 Cook noodles in large saucepan of boiling water until tender, drain. Rinse under cold water; drain.
3 Meanwhile, discard mushroom stalks. Place mushroom caps in small heatproof bowl, cover with boiling water; stand 15 minutes or until softened. Drain then slice mushrooms.
4 Toss noodles and mushrooms with remaining ingredients and dressing in large bowl.
mirin and tamari dressing Combine ingredients in screw-top jar, shake well.
prep + cook time *30 minutes (+ standing)*
serves *4*
nutritional count per serving *1.8g total fat (0.2g saturated fat); 1124kJ (269 cal); 47.9g carbohydrate; 11.2g protein; 5g fibre*

Detoxing occasionally for a short time makes you feel great, especially if you've been over-indulging for a while. Eat less, and eat light in-season fruit and vegetables as well as a little poultry or fish. Don't eat over-processed carbs, and avoid red meat, alcohol and caffeine drinks.

WATERCRESS AND PINEAPPLE SOOTHER

Using an electric juicer, extract juice from 2 cups firmly packed watercress sprigs, 2 coarsely chopped trimmed celery stalks, ½ peeled and chopped medium pineapple and 2cm piece peeled fresh ginger.

prep time *15 minutes* serves *2*
nutritional count per serving *0.6g total fat (0g saturated fat); 443kJ (106 cal); 15.9g carbohydrate; 4.7g protein; 8.5g fibre*

BETA-CAROTENE KICK START

Using an electric juicer, extract juice from 1 peeled and coarsely chopped medium pear, ½ cup firmly packed fresh flat-leaf parsley leaves, 2 coarsely chopped medium carrots and ¼ small peeled, seeded and coarsely chopped rockmelon.

prep time *15 minutes* serves *2*
nutritional count per serving *0.4g total fat (0g saturated fat); 497kJ (119 cal); 24g carbohydrate; 2g protein; 7.3g fibre*

detoxing food

CHLOROPHYLL AND BEETROOT CLEANSER

Using an electric juicer, extract juice from 2 coarsely chopped trimmed celery stalks, 1 coarsely chopped medium apple, ½ cup firmly packed fresh flat-leaf parsley leaves, 1 peeled and coarsely chopped large orange and 1 peeled small beetroot.
prep time *15 minutes* serves *2*
nutritional count per serving *0.3g total fat (0g saturated fat); 468kJ (112 cal); 20.9g carbohydrate; 3g protein; 7.2g fibre*

CARROT, ORANGE AND GARLIC JUICE

Using an electric juicer, extract juice from 3 coarsely chopped medium carrots, 2 peeled and coarsely chopped large oranges, 1 peeled small clove garlic and 2cm piece peeled fresh ginger.
prep time *15 minutes* serves *2*
nutritional count per serving *0.4g total fat (0g saturated fat); 581kJ (139 cal); 25.5g carbohydrate; 3.5g protein; 9.2g fibre*

detoxing food

ROAST VEGETABLES WITH LENTILS

400g baby carrots, trimmed

350g pumpkin, cut into 2cm wedges

4 small egg tomatoes (240g), halved

1 small red onion (80g), cut into 8 wedges

2 flat mushrooms (160g), halved

1 clove garlic, crushed

1 tablespoon olive oil

2 tablespoons balsamic vinegar

½ cup walnuts (50g), chopped coarsely

400g can brown lentils, rinsed, drained

¼ cup finely chopped fresh flat-leaf parsley

1 Preheat oven to 220°C/200°C fan-forced. Line large baking dish with baking paper.

2 Place vegetables, in single layer, in baking dish. Combine garlic, oil and vinegar in small bowl; pour over vegetables. Roast about 30 minutes or until vegetables are tender. Cool 10 minutes.

3 Combine vegetables in large bowl with nuts, lentils and parsley.

prep + cook time *45 minutes* serves 4
nutritional count per serving *14g total fat (1.4g saturated fat); 1045kJ (250 cal); 17.3g carbohydrate; 9.5g protein; 8.5g fibre*

RAW VEGETABLE SUMMER SALAD

2 tablespoons red wine vinegar

1 tablespoon macadamia oil

1 tablespoon water

1 medium avocado (250g), chopped finely

8 button mushrooms (120g), sliced thinly

2 lebanese cucumbers (260g), chopped coarsely

1 medium yellow capsicum (200g), sliced thinly

1 medium tomato (150g), chopped finely

½ cup small fresh basil leaves

12 small baby cos lettuce leaves

1 Whisk vinegar, oil and the water in medium bowl. Add avocado, mushrooms, cucumber, capsicum, tomato and basil; toss gently.
2 Serve salad with lettuce leaves.
prep time *20 minutes* serves 4
nutritional count per serving *14.2g total fat (2.8g saturated fat); 686kJ (164 cal); 3.7g carbohydrate; 3.4g protein; 3.7g fibre*

detoxing food

APPLE AND SEED SLAW WITH MACADAMIA DRESSING

1 medium apple (150g), cut into matchsticks

2 tablespoons lemon juice

50g snow pea sprouts, chopped coarsely

½ cup (50g) fresh mung beans

¼ medium wombok (250g), shredded finely

1 medium carrot (120g), grated coarsely

6 green onions, sliced thinly

¼ cup finely chopped fresh chives

2 tablespoons sunflower seed kernels

2 tablespoons pepitas

macadamia dressing

2 tablespoons lemon juice

1 tablespoon macadamia oil

1 Make macadamia dressing.
2 Combine apple and lemon juice in large bowl. Add remaining ingredients and dressing to bowl; toss gently.
macadamia dressing Combine ingredients in screw-top jar; shake well.
prep time *30 minutes* serves *4*
nutritional count per serving *9g total fat (1.2g saturated fat); 627kJ (150 cal); 10.2g carbohydrate; 4.8g protein; 4.1g fibre*

Pepitas are pumpkin seeds. They are a good source of zinc and iron, and can be sprinkled on salads, vegie dishes or even your breakfast cereal to add an extra nutritional burst.

detoxing food

76

detoxing food

GRAPEFRUIT, HONEYDEW AND BABY ENDIVE SALAD

2 medium grapefruit (850g), peeled

1 tablespoon flaxseed oil

1 tablespoon water

170g asparagus, halved lengthways, chopped coarsely

¼ large honeydew melon (425g), peeled, seeded, sliced thinly lengthways

120g baby endive leaves

60g baby spinach leaves

4 green onions, sliced thinly

2 tablespoons pepitas

1 Segment grapefruit over small bowl; reserve ¼ cup juice. Combine reserved juice with oil and water in large bowl; whisk well. Add grapefruit segments to bowl.

2 Boil, steam or microwave asparagus until tender. Rinse under cold water, drain.

3 Add asparagus to grapefruit mixture with remaining ingredients; toss gently.

prep + cook time *15 minutes* serves 4
nutritional count per serving *7.9g total fat (0.9g saturated fat); 644kJ (154 cal); 13.2g carbohydrate; 5.1g protein; 3.9g fibre*

BROWN RICE AND SPLIT PEA SALAD WITH ORANGE DRESSING

¾ cup (150g) brown long-grain rice

¾ cup (150g) green split peas

150g snow peas, sliced thinly

2 small zucchini (180g), sliced thinly

1 medium red capsicum (200g), chopped finely

80g baby spinach leaves, shredded coarsely

orange dressing

⅓ cup (80ml) strained freshly squeezed
   orange juice

1 small clove garlic, crushed

2 teaspoons sesame oil

1 Make orange dressing.

2 Cook rice and split peas in medium saucepan of boiling water about 20 minutes or until tender. Drain; rinse under cold water, drain.

3 Add snow peas to medium saucepan of boiling water; return to the boil. Drain; rinse under cold water, drain.

4 Combine rice mixture with snow peas, remaining ingredients and dressing in large bowl; toss gently.

orange dressing Combine ingredients in screw-top jar; shake well.

prep + cook time *30 minutes* serves 4
nutritional count per serving 4.3g total fat
(0.6g saturated fat); 1346kJ (322 cal);
52.4g carbohydrate; 14.5g protein; 7.8g fibre

detoxing food

79

FOOD FOR STRENGTH AND LONGEVITY

BEEF WITH RED WINE AND KUMARA MASH

4 cloves garlic

3 cups (750ml) dry red wine

2 cups (500ml) water

8 sprigs fresh thyme

600g piece middle-cut beef eye fillet, trimmed,
   tied at 3cm intervals

kumara mash

1 large (500g) kumara, unpeeled

¼ cup (60ml) fresh orange juice, strained

1 teaspoon fresh thyme leaves

1 Bruise unpeeled garlic by hitting with the flat blade of a heavy knife.
2 Combine garlic, wine, the water and thyme in large deep saucepan; bring to the boil, boil 5 minutes. Add beef; simmer, uncovered, about 30 minutes or until cooked as desired, turning beef once. Remove beef, wrap in foil; stand 10 minutes.
3 Meanwhile make kumara mash.
4 Slice beef; serve with kumara mash and wholegrain mustard.
kumara mash Boil, steam or microwave kumara until tender; cool. Peel kumara; place in large saucepan, roughly mash. Add juice and thyme; stir over medium heat until hot. Season to taste.

prep + cook time *30 minutes* serves *4*
nutritional count per serving *4.7g total fat (1.7g saturated fat); 1605kJ (384 cal); 16.4g carbohydrate; 36.1g protein; 2.5g fibre*

The beef will be medium-rare if cooked for 20 minutes.

Eat meals that contain a variety of fresh food and avoid high-fat food and food that has been over-processed. The nearer the food is to its natural state, the better it is for your health, well-being and longevity.

THAI BEEF SALAD WITH RICE NOODLES

400g piece lean rump steak

100g thin dried rice stick noodles

1 telegraph cucumber (400g), peeled, seeded, chopped coarsely

½ cup (70g) unsalted peanuts, roasted

250g cherry tomatoes, halved

1 tablespoon finely chopped lemon grass

½ cup loosely packed fresh coriander leaves

½ cup loosely packed fresh thai basil leaves

2 fresh long red chillies, sliced thinly

lime dressing

¼ cup (60ml) fish sauce

¼ cup (60ml) lime juice

½ teaspoon caster sugar

1 clove garlic, crushed

1 Cook beef in heated oiled medium frying pan until browned both sides. Cover beef; stand 10 minutes then slice thinly.
2 Meanwhile, make lime dressing.
3 Place noodles in large heatproof bowl; cover with boiling water. Stand noodles until tender, drain.
4 Combine beef with noodles, dressing and remaining ingredients in large bowl. Season to taste.
lime dressing Combine ingredients in small bowl.
prep + cook time *30 minutes* serves *4*
nutritional count per serving *13.2g total fat (2.7g saturated fat); 1175kJ (281 cal); 10.6g carbohydrate; 27.7g protein; 3.9g fibre*

For easier serving and eating, cut noodles into shorter lengths with scissors.

food for strength and longevity

CHICKEN AND RED LENTIL DHAL

1 tablespoon olive oil

1 medium brown onion (150g), sliced finely

2 cloves garlic, crushed

2 fresh long green chillies, sliced thinly

2 teaspoons ground cumin

2 teaspoons ground coriander

2 teaspoons ground turmeric

1 cup dried red lentils (200g), rinsed

500g chicken stir-fry strips

3 cups (750ml) water

250g broccoli florets

1 cup **loosely** packed fresh coriander leaves

⅓ cup (95g) yogurt

1 lemon (140g), cut into wedges

1 Heat oil in large saucepan; cook onion and garlic, stirring, until onion is browned lightly. Add chilli and spices; cook, stirring, until fragrant. Add lentils, chicken and the water; bring to the boil. Reduce heat; simmer, uncovered, 15 minutes. Add broccoli; simmer, covered, about 5 minutes or until broccoli is tender and liquid absorbed. Season to taste.

2 Sprinkle with coriander; serve with yogurt and lemon wedges.

prep + cook time *35 minutes* serves *4*
nutritional count per serving *8.4g total fat (1.8g saturated fat); 1555kJ (372 cal); 23.6g carbohydrate; 45.2g protein; 11g fibre*

food for strength and longevity

PEPPERED STEAK WITH TOMATO AND ROCKET SALAD

600g piece middle-cut beef eye fillet, trimmed

2 teaspoons dijon mustard

2 teaspoons cracked black pepper

tomato and rocket salad

1 tablespoon red wine vinegar

1 tablespoon olive oil

250g baby egg tomatoes, halved

100g yellow grape tomatoes, halved

3 small kumatoes (270g), sliced thinly (*see tip*)

60g baby rocket

1 Preheat oven to 220°C/200°C fan-forced.
2 Coat beef in mustard and pepper. Heat large oiled frying pan; brown beef all over.
3 Place beef into heated oiled baking dish; transfer to oven. Roast beef, uncovered, about 20 minutes or until cooked as desired. Cover loosely with foil; stand 10 minutes.
4 Meanwhile, make tomato and rocket salad.
5 Slice beef; serve with salad.

tomato and rocket salad Whisk vinegar and oil in large bowl. Add remaining ingredients; toss gently. Season to taste.

prep + cook time *35 minutes* serves 4
nutritional count per serving *9.4g total fat (2.3g saturated fat); 1028kJ (246 cal); 3.4g carbohydrate; 35.4g protein; 2.2g fibre*

If kumatoes aren't available any tomato will do.

food for strength and longevity

84

FISH, WHITE BEAN AND TOMATO STEW

1 tablespoon olive oil

3 stalks celery (450g), trimmed, chopped finely

3 cloves garlic, crushed

1 medium brown onion (150g), chopped finely

2 x 400g cans cherry tomatoes in tomato juice

1½ cups (375ml) salt-reduced chicken stock

400g can cannellini beans, rinsed, drained

400g can butter beans, rinsed, drained

600g skinless firm white fish fillets, cut into 4cm pieces

½ cup coarsely chopped fresh flat-leaf parsley

1 Heat oil in large saucepan; cook celery, garlic and onion, stirring, until onion is soft. Add undrained tomatoes, stock and beans; bring to the boil. Reduce heat; simmer, uncovered, 10 minutes.

2 Add fish to pan; simmer, uncovered, about 10 minutes or until fish is cooked. Serve sprinkled with parsley.

prep + cook time *35 minutes* serves 4
nutritional count per serving *9.1g total fat (2g saturated fat); 1400kJ (335 cal); 19.2g carbohydrate; 39.6g protein; 9.5g fibre*

We used blue-eye trevalla for this recipe.

food for strength and longevity

CRUMBED CHICKEN WITH CITRUS SALAD

½ cup (80g) almond kernels, chopped finely

⅓ cup (35g) wheat germ

2 tablespoons finely chopped fresh
   flat-leaf parsley

900g chicken tenderloins

2 egg whites, beaten lightly

citrus salad

1 ruby red grapefruit (350g)

2 medium oranges (480g)

1 teaspoon dijon mustard

2 teaspoons vegetable oil

2 cups (230g) firmly packed watercress sprigs

1 shallot (25g), thinly sliced

1 Preheat oven to 220°C/200°C fan-forced. Line oven tray with baking paper.

2 Combine nuts, wheat germ and parsley in medium bowl. Dip chicken into egg white, then in almond mixture; place on tray. Roast, uncovered, about 12 minutes or until chicken is browned and cooked through.

3 Meanwhile make citrus salad.

4 Serve chicken with salad. Season to taste.

citrus salad Peel and segment grapefruit and oranges over large bowl to collect juice. Whisk mustard and oil into juice in bowl. Add watercress, shallot and citrus segments; toss gently. Season to taste.

prep + cook time *30 minutes* serves 6
nutritional count per serving *11.9g total fat (1.5g saturated fat); 1313kJ (314 cal); 9.3g carbohydrate; 40g protein; 4.1g fibre*

This citrus salad is loaded with vitamin C and is a wonderful sharp addition to the lean and protein-packed crunchy chicken.

BRAISED CHICKEN WITH CHICKPEAS, LEMON AND GARLIC

1 tablespoon olive oil

2 medium brown onions (300g), sliced thickly

2 teaspoons smoked paprika

3 cloves garlic, crushed

8 chicken thigh cutlets, skin removed (1.6kg)

3 cups (750ml) salt-reduced chicken stock

¼ cup (60ml) lemon juice

2 fresh long red chillies, halved lengthways

2 x 400g cans chickpeas, rinsed, drained

2 teaspoons dijon mustard

½ cup coarsely chopped fresh flat-leaf parsley

2 teaspoons finely grated lemon rind

1 Heat oil in large saucepan; cook onion, stirring, until softened. Add paprika, garlic and chicken; stir to coat chicken in onion mixture.

2 Add stock, juice, chilli, chickpeas and mustard to pan; bring to the boil. Reduce heat; simmer, covered, 30 minutes. Uncover; simmer about 30 minutes or until chicken is tender.

3 Serve sprinkled with parsley and rind.

prep + cook time *1 hour 15 minutes* serves 4
nutritional count per serving *22.4g total fat (5.6g saturated fat); 2378kJ (569 cal); 24.7g carbohydrate; 63.5g protein; 8.4g fibre*

KECAP MANIS FISH AND MUSHROOM SKEWERS

2 tablespoons salt-reduced soy sauce

¼ cup (60ml) kecap manis

2 cloves garlic, crushed

3 green onions, chopped finely

600g skinless white fish fillet, cut into 2.5cm pieces

8 medium swiss brown mushrooms (180g), halved

600g buk choy, chopped coarsely

2 tablespoons water

1 lime, cut into wedges

1 Combine sauces, garlic and onion in large bowl; add fish and mushrooms. Thread mushrooms and fish onto eight skewers. Reserve marinade.
2 Cook skewers, in batches, in heated oiled large frying pan. Remove from pan; cover to keep warm.
3 Add buk choy, reserved marinade and the water to same pan; bring to the boil. Reduce heat, simmer until buk choy is wilted. Season to taste.
4 Serve buk choy mixture with skewers; accompany with lime wedges.

prep + cook time *25 minutes* serves 4
nutritional count per serving *3.8g total fat (1.1g saturated fat); 882kJ (211 cal); 2.7g carbohydrate; 37.8g protein; 5.5g fibre*

Soak bamboo skewers in water for at least 30 minutes to prevent burning during cooking. We used ling fillets in this recipe.

FELAFEL WITH KUMARA HUMMUS

2 x 400g cans chickpeas, rinsed, drained

4 green onions, chopped coarsely

½ cup (60g) frozen peas, thawed

2 teaspoons ground cumin

2 teaspoons ground coriander

¼ cup (40g) wholemeal spelt flour

2 egg whites

2 teaspoons bicarbonate of soda

kumara hummus

1 small kumara (250g), chopped coarsely

400g can chickpeas, rinsed, drained

2 tablespoons tahini

2 cloves garlic, chopped coarsely

¼ cup (60ml) lemon juice

¼ cup (60ml) water

1 Make kumara hummus.
2 Process ingredients until smooth; season to taste. Place heaped tablespoons of mixture onto baking-paper-lined trays; cover, refrigerate 2 hours.
3 With wet hands, shape mixture into patties. Cook patties, turning gently, in heated oiled large frying pan, in batches, until felafels are browned both sides.
4 Serve felafels with kumara hummus.
kumara hummus Boil, steam or microwave kumara until tender; drain. Process kumara with remaining ingredients until smooth. Season to taste.
prep + cook time *40 minutes (+ refrigeration)*
serves 6
nutritional count per serving *7.3g total fat (0.9g saturated fat); 1028kJ (246 cal); 27.4g carbohydrate; 13.6g protein; 9.4g fibre*

Serve with a cucumber and rocket salad.

TUNA WITH QUINOA AND BROWN RICE PILAF

1½ cups (300g) brown long-grain rice

1 tablespoon olive oil

1 medium red onion (170g), chopped finely

2 teaspoons brown mustard seeds

3 teaspoons garam masala

½ cup (100g) quinoa

2 cups (500ml) salt-reduced chicken stock

1 cup (250ml) water

2 fresh long green chillies, sliced thinly

2 tablespoons lemon juice

2 skinless tuna steaks (350g), chopped finely

80g baby spinach leaves, shredded coarsely

½ cup loosely packed fresh coriander leaves

1 lemon, cut into wedges

1 Boil, steam or microwave rice until tender; drain.
2 Heat oil in large saucepan; cook onion, seeds and garam masala, stirring, until onion is soft. Add quinoa, stock, the water and half the chilli; bring to the boil. Reduce heat; simmer, covered, 15 minutes.
3 Add rice, juice, tuna and spinach; cook, stirring, 2 minutes or until rice is hot. Season to taste.
4 Serve tuna mixture with remaining chilli, coriander and lemon wedges.

prep + cook time *35 minutes* serves 4
nutritional count per serving *12.7g total fat (3.4g saturated fat); 2458kJ (588 cal); 81.7g carbohydrate; 32.6g protein; 5.2g fibre*

Quinoa (keen-wa) is the seed of a leafy plant similar to spinach. Its cooking qualities are similar to rice, and it has a slightly nutty taste and chewy texture; keep quinoa sealed in a glass jar under refrigeration because it spoils easily. Available from health-food stores.

GLUTEN-FREE PASTA WITH FRESH TOMATO SAUCE

375g gluten-free fettuccine pasta

1kg egg tomatoes, chopped coarsely

1½ tablespoons olive oil

½ cup (80g) blanched almonds, chopped coarsely

2 cloves garlic, crushed

½ cup firmly packed fresh basil leaves

½ teaspoon dried chilli flakes

½ cup (60g) seeded black olives, chopped coarsely

½ cup (120g) low-fat ricotta cheese

1 Cook pasta in large saucepan of boiling water until tender; drain, reserve ⅓ cup cooking liquid.

2 Meanwhile, combine tomato, oil, nuts, garlic, basil, chilli and olives in large bowl.

3 Add pasta and reserved cooking liquid to tomato mixture; toss gently. Season to taste.

4 Serve pasta topped with teaspoons of ricotta.

prep + cook time *35 minutes* serves 4

nutritional count per serving *23g total fat (3.3g saturated fat); 2521kJ (603 cal); 73.8g carbohydrate; 17g protein; 15.7g fibre*

food for strength and longevity

BROCCOLINI, BROWN RICE AND SESAME STIR-FRY

⅔ cup (130g) brown long-grain rice

350g broccolini, trimmed

3 cloves garlic, crushed

6 green onions, sliced thinly

2 fresh long red chillies, sliced thinly

1 medium red capsicum (200g), sliced thinly

2 teaspoons sesame oil

2 tablespoons light soy sauce

2 tablespoons water

½ cup (70g) macadamias, chopped coarsely

1 Boil, steam or microwave rice until tender; drain, cool.

2 Cut broccolini stems in half lengthways, then in half crossways.

3 Stir-fry garlic, onion, chilli and capsicum in heated oiled wok 1 minute. Add oil, broccolini and rice; stir-fry 1 minute. Add sauce and the water; stir-fry about 2 minutes or until broccolini is tender. Season to taste. Serve sprinkled with nuts.

prep + cook time *15 minutes* serves 4
nutritional count per serving 16.9g total fat
(2.3g saturated fat); 1346kJ (322 cal);
29.3g carbohydrate; 9.7g protein; 7g fibre

food for strength and longevity

93

GLUTEN-FREE DESSERTS & CAKES

LEMON AND ALMOND SYRUP CAKES

80g butter, softened

½ cup (110g) caster sugar

3 eggs

1½ cups (180g) ground almonds

⅓ cup (60g) rice flour

2 tablespoons flaked almonds

lemon syrup

½ cup (125ml) lemon juice

½ cup (125ml) water

½ cup (110g) caster sugar

1 Preheat oven to 180°C/160°C fan forced. Grease 6-hole (½-cup/125ml) oval friand pan.
2 Beat butter and sugar in small bowl with electric mixer until light and fluffy. Beat in eggs, one at a time (mixture will curdle at this stage, but will come together later). Stir in ground almonds and flour. Divide mixture into pan holes; sprinkle with flaked nuts. Bake about 25 minutes.
3 Meanwhile, make lemon syrup.
4 Stand cakes in pan 5 minutes before turning, top-side up, onto wire rack over tray. Pour hot lemon syrup over hot cakes.
lemon syrup Combine ingredients in small saucepan; stir over heat until sugar dissolves. Bring to the boil. Boil, uncovered, without stirring, about 10 minutes or until syrup thickens. Pour syrup into small heatproof jug.
prep + cook time 40 minutes makes 6
nutritional count per cake 31.6g total fat (9.3g saturated fat); 2140kJ (512 cal); 46.9g carbohydrate; 10.9g protein; 2.9g fibre

Gluten is a protein found mostly in wheat, and many people are intolerant to it. While gluten-free main-course recipes are easy to find, there are fewer options for desserts and sweet treats. We've remedied that situation with the recipes in this chapter.

BANANA BREAD

1¼ cups (170g) gluten-free self-raising flour

1 teaspoon ground cinnamon

20g butter

1 egg

¼ cup (60ml) milk

½ cup (110g) firmly packed brown sugar

½ cup mashed banana

1 tablespoon pepitas

2 teaspoons sunflower seed kernels

2 medium bananas (400g), sliced

⅔ cup (160g) ricotta cheese

⅓ cup (115g) honey

1 Preheat oven to 220°C/200°C fan forced. Grease 8cm x 20cm loaf pan; line base with baking paper.
2 Sift flour and cinnamon into large bowl; rub in butter. Whisk egg and milk in small bowl; stir into flour mixture with sugar and mashed banana. (Do not overmix, the batter should be lumpy.) Pour mixture into pan; sprinkle with seeds. Bake bread about 35 minutes.
3 Stand in pan 10 minutes before turning, top-side up, onto wire rack to cool.
4 Cut bread into eight slices. Toast lightly; serve with sliced banana, ricotta and honey.
prep + cook time *40 minutes* serves *8*
nutritional count per serving *6.7g total fat (3.4g saturated fat); 1208kJ (289 cal); 50.6g carbohydrate; 6.8g protein; 2.1g fibre*

Uncut banana bread will keep in an airtight container for up to two days. Banana bread is suitable to freeze for up to three months. You will need one large overripe banana to get ½ cup mashed banana.

STRAWBERRY JAM DROPS

100g butter, softened

½ cup (110g) caster sugar

1 egg white

1 cup (120g) ground almonds

⅓ cup (50g) potato flour

⅓ cup (50g) cornflour (100% corn)

pure icing sugar for dusting, optional

strawberry jam

250g strawberries

1½ tablespoons lemon juice

1 cup (220g) caster sugar

1 Make strawberry jam.

2 Preheat oven to 180°C/160°C fan forced. Line two greased oven trays with baking paper.

3 Stir butter, sugar, egg white and ground almonds in small bowl until combined. Stir in sifted flours.

4 Drop level tablespoons of mixture onto trays, 5cm apart. Using handle of a wooden spoon, make a 1cm indentation in centre of each biscuit. Fill each indentation with ¼ teaspoon of the jam. Bake about 15 minutes or until browned lightly. Cool on trays. Dust with sifted icing sugar.

strawberry jam Combine strawberries and juice in medium microwave-safe bowl; microwave on HIGH (100%) 4 minutes. Stir in sugar; microwave on HIGH, stirring occasionally, about 12 minutes or until jam jells when tested on a cold saucer. Stand 5 minutes; pour into hot sterilised jar. Seal while hot.

prep + cook time *1 hour (+ cooling)* **makes** *20* **nutritional count per biscuit** *7.4g total fat (2.9g saturated fat); 656kJ (157 cal); 21.4g carbohydrate; 1.6g protein; 0.7g fibre*

Use bought jam if you prefer not to make it.

MOIST APPLE WALNUT SLICE WITH MAPLE SYRUP ICING

3 medium apples (450g)

1 cup (150g) potato flour

¾ cup (120g) brown rice flour

¼ cup (30g) ground walnuts

1 cup (220g) caster sugar

1 teaspoon bicarbonate of soda

4 eggs, beaten lightly

1 cup (250ml) vegetable oil

½ cup (55g) coarsely chopped walnuts

maple syrup icing

1½ cups (240g) pure icing sugar

1½ tablespoons hot water

1 tablespoon maple syrup

1 Preheat oven to 180°C/160°C fan-forced. Grease 19cm x 30cm lamington pan; line base with baking paper, extending paper 5cm over two long sides.
2 Peel apples; grate coarsely.
3 Sift dry ingredients into large bowl; stir in apple, eggs and oil. Pour mixture into pan; bake about 40 minutes. Stand slice in pan 10 minutes before turning, top-side up, onto wire rack to cool.
4 Make maple syrup icing. Spread slice with icing; sprinkle with chopped walnuts.

maple syrup icing Sift icing sugar into small bowl; stir in the hot water and maple syrup.

prep + cook time *55 minutes* serves *18*
nutritional count per serving *17.6g total fat (2.3g saturated fat); 1379kJ (330 cal); 40.3g carbohydrate; 3.8g protein; 1.1g fibre*

To ground walnuts, blend or process until fine. Store slice in an airtight container for up to three days. Un-iced slice is suitable to freeze for up to three months.

Walnuts are full of omega-3 essential fatty acids, the good fat that we all need in our diets. They also add a wonderful flavour and extra crunch to this delicious slice.

CRANBERRY AND HONEY MUESLI BARS

125g butter, chopped coarsely

⅓ cup (75g) firmly packed brown sugar

2 tablespoons honey

1½ cups (165g) rolled rice

½ cup (65g) gluten-free self-raising flour

⅓ cup (45g) dried cranberries, chopped finely

⅓ cup (50g) finely chopped seeded dried dates

⅓ cup (55g) sultanas, chopped finely

¼ cup (50g) pepitas

2 tablespoons sesame seeds

1 Preheat oven to 160°C/140°C fan-forced. Grease 19cm x 29cm slice pan; line base with baking paper, extending paper 5cm over long sides.
2 Combine butter, sugar and honey in small saucepan; stir over low heat until smooth.
3 Combine remaining ingredients in large bowl; stir in butter mixture. Press mixture firmly into pan; bake, in oven, about 35 minutes or until golden brown. Cool in pan before cutting into bars.
prep + cook time *40 minutes (+ cooling)*
makes *15*
nutritional count per bar *10.3g total fat (5.2g saturated fat); 857kJ (205 cal); 24.9g carbohydrate; 3g protein; 2.4g fibre*

MACADAMIA AND CRANBERRY WAFERS

2 egg whites

⅓ cup (75g) caster sugar

½ cup (65g) gluten-free plain flour

1 teaspoon finely grated lemon rind

½ cup (70g) macadamias

½ cup (65g) dried cranberries

1 Preheat oven to 180°C/160°C fan forced. Grease 8cm x 26cm bar cake pan; line base with baking paper.

2 Beat egg whites in small bowl with electric mixer until soft peaks form. Gradually add sugar, beating until sugar is dissolved between additions; transfer mixture to medium bowl.

3 Fold sifted flour and rind into egg-white mixture then fold in nuts and cranberries; spread into pan. Bake about 30 minutes; cool in pan. Wrap bar in foil; refrigerate 3 hours or overnight.

4 Preheat oven to 150°C/130°C fan-forced. Line oven trays with baking paper.

5 Using serrated or electric knife, cut bread into 3mm slices; place, in single layer, on trays. Bake about 15 minutes or until crisp.

prep + cook time *1 hour (+ refrigeration)*
makes *38*
nutritional count per wafer *1.4g total fat (0.2g saturated fat); 138kJ (33 cal); 4.4g carbohydrate; 0.5g protein; 0.3g fibre*

Wafers can be stored in an airtight container for up to 1 week.

gluten-free desserts & cakes

101

CUSTARD TART

90g butter, softened

¼ cup (55g) caster sugar

1 egg

1¼ cups (170g) gluten-free plain flour

¼ cup (35g) gluten-free self-raising flour

1 egg white

1 tablespoon pure icing sugar

125g raspberries

vanilla custard

3 eggs

1 teaspoon vanilla extract

2 tablespoons caster sugar

2 cups (500ml) hot milk

1 Beat butter and sugar in small bowl with electric mixer until combined. Add egg; beat until combined. Stir in sifted flours, in two batches; turn pastry onto floured surface, knead lightly until smooth. Cover, refrigerate 30 minutes.

2 Preheat oven to 180°C/160°C fan-forced. Grease 20cm pie dish.

3 Roll pastry between two sheets of baking paper until large enough to line dish. Ease pastry into dish, press into base and side; trim edge. Brush base and sides of pastry with egg white; place pie dish on oven tray.

4 Make vanilla custard.

5 Pour vanilla custard into pastry. Bake about 50 minutes or until browned lightly. Cool.

6 To serve, dust tart with sifted icing sugar; serve with raspberries.

vanilla custard Whisk eggs, extract and sugar in medium bowl; gradually whisk in milk. Strain egg mixture through fine sieve into large heatproof jug.

prep + cook time *1 hour 20 minutes (+ refrigeration)* serves *8*

nutritional count per serving *15g total fat (8.7g saturated fat); 1308kJ (313 cal); 35g carbohydrate; 9.3g protein; 1.8g fibre*

We used a pie dish 20cm wide at the base for this recipe. Do not overcook as the custard will become firm as it cools. The custard tart is best eaten at room temperature.

MIXED BERRY AND APPLE PUDDINGS

⅓ cup (110g) mixed berry jam

1 medium apple (150g)

1 egg

½ cup (110g) caster sugar

1 cup (135g) gluten-free self-raising flour

½ cup (125ml) milk

20g butter, melted

1 tablespoon boiling water

1 teaspoon vanilla extract

1 Grease four 1-cup (250ml) metal moulds; divide jam into moulds.

2 Peel apple; grate coarsely. Squeeze and discard excess liquid from apple.

3 Beat egg and sugar in small bowl with electric mixer until thick and creamy. Fold in sifted flour, then milk, apple, butter, the water and extract.

4 Spoon pudding mixture into moulds. Cover each mould with pleated baking paper and foil; secure with string.

5 Place puddings in large saucepan with enough boiling water to come half way up sides of moulds. Cover pan with tight-fitting lid; boil 25 minutes, replenishing with boiling water as necessary. Stand puddings 5 minutes before turning onto plates. Serve warm.

prep + cook time *40 minutes (+ standing)*
serves 4

nutritional count per serving *7.2g total fat (4g saturated fat); 1605kJ (384 cal); 74.2g carbohydrate; 6.5g protein; 2.2g fibre*

gluten-free desserts & cakes

CHOCOLATE FUDGE CAKES WITH COFFEE SYRUP

½ cup (50g) cocoa powder

1 cup (220g) firmly packed brown sugar

½ cup (125ml) boiling water

100g dark eating chocolate, chopped finely

2 egg yolks

¼ cup (30g) ground almonds

2 tablespoons potato flour

2 tablespoons brown rice flour

4 egg whites

coffee syrup

¾ cup (165g) firmly packed brown sugar

¾ cup (180ml) water

1 tablespoon instant coffee granules

1 Preheat oven to 160°C/140°C fan forced. Butter a 12-hole (½-cup/125ml) friand pan.

2 Sift cocoa and sugar into large bowl; stir in the water then chocolate until smooth. Stir in egg yolks, ground almonds and sifted flours.

3 Beat egg whites in small bowl with electric mixer until soft peaks form. Fold whites into chocolate mixture in two batches; drop ⅓ cup (80ml) mixture into pan holes. Bake about 20 minutes.

4 Meanwhile, make coffee syrup.

5 Stand cakes in pan 5 minutes before turning, top-side up, onto serving plates; serve drizzled with hot coffee syrup.

coffee syrup Stir sugar and the water in small saucepan over heat until sugar dissolves; bring to the boil. Reduce heat; simmer, uncovered, without stirring, about 15 minutes or until syrup thickens. Stir in coffee; strain into small heatproof jug.

*prep + cook time 35 minutes makes 12
nutritional count per serving 5.2g total fat
(2.1g saturated fat); 899kJ (215 cal);
40.1g carbohydrate; 3.5g protein; 0.6g fibre*

Don't worry too much about delicately folding in the egg whites; the heavy chocolate mixture will flatten the egg whites. Cakes can be frozen for up to a month; reheat in a microwave oven. The syrup can be made a week ahead; keep, covered, in the fridge.

gluten-free desserts & cakes

105

CRÊPES WITH CRANBERRY ORANGE SAUCE

¾ cup (100g) gluten-free plain flour

3 eggs

2 tablespoons vegetable oil

¾ cup (180ml) milk

pure icing sugar for dusting, optional

cranberry orange sauce

¼ cup (55g) caster sugar

1 cinnamon stick

⅓ cup (80ml) orange juice

⅓ cup (50g) frozen cranberries

1 Sift flour into medium bowl, add eggs and oil; gradually whisk in milk until smooth. Pour batter into large jug, cover; stand 1 hour.

2 Heat oiled heavy-based crêpe pan or small frying pan; pour in ¼ cup of batter, tilt pan to coat base. Cook crêpe over low heat until browned lightly, loosening around edge with spatula. Turn crêpe; brown other side. Remove crêpe from pan; cover. Repeat to make a total of eight crepes.

3 Make cranberry orange sauce.

4 Fold crêpes in half then in half again; place on serving plates. Pour hot sauce over crêpes. Dust with sifted icing sugar before serving.

cranberry orange sauce Combine sugar, cinnamon and juice in small saucepan; stir over heat until sugar dissolves. Bring to the boil; boil, uncovered, without stirring, 2 minutes. Add cranberries; simmer, uncovered, 2 minutes. Remove from heat; stand 5 minutes. Discard cinnamon.

prep + cook time *35 minutes (+ standing)*
serves *4*
nutritional count per serving *15.8g total fat (3.7g saturated fat); 1371kJ (328 cal); 36.3g carbohydrate; 10.1g protein; 1.7g fibre*

These little berries are not only scrumptious on crêpes, but they also have a number of health benefits, including being full of antioxidants and antibacterial properties.

BUCKWHEAT PANCAKES WITH CARAMELISED BANANAS

½ cup (65g) gluten-free self-raising flour

½ cup (75g) buckwheat flour

1 tablespoon caster sugar

¼ teaspoon ground cinnamon

1 egg

¾ cup (180ml) milk

20g butter

¼ cup (55g) firmly packed brown sugar

4 medium bananas (800g), sliced thickly

⅓ cup (80ml) hot water

1 Sift flours, caster sugar and cinnamon into medium bowl. Whisk in egg and milk until batter is smooth.

2 Melt butter in large frying pan. Add brown sugar; cook, stirring, until dissolved. Add banana and half the water; cook, uncovered, stirring occasionally, about 2 minutes or until banana is caramelised.

3 Pour 2 level tablespoons of batter into heated oiled medium frying pan; cook until browned both sides. Remove from pan; cover. Repeat to make a total of eight pancakes.

4 Divide pancakes between serving plates; top with banana. Add the remaining water to caramel in frying pan; stir to combine, pour over pancakes.

prep + cook time *30 minutes* serves 4
nutritional count per serving *8.1g total fat (4.4g saturated fat); 1630kJ (390 cal); 68.2g carbohydrate; 9.6g protein; 5.9g fibre*

gluten-free desserts & cakes

GOLDEN SYRUP STEAMED PUDDING

60g butter

¼ cup (90g) golden syrup

½ teaspoon bicarbonate of soda

½ cup (125ml) milk

1 egg

1 cup (135g) gluten-free self-raising flour

2 teaspoons ground ginger

syrup

⅓ cup (115g) golden syrup

2 tablespoons water

30g butter

1 Grease 1-litre (4-cup) pudding bowl or steamer.
2 Melt butter with syrup in small saucepan; remove from heat, stir in soda. Pour into medium bowl; stir in combined milk and egg then sifted flour and ginger.
3 Pour mixture into pudding bowl. Cover with pleated baking paper and foil; secure with string.
4 Place bowl in large saucepan with enough boiling water to come half way up side of bowl; cover with tight-fitting lid. Boil 1 hour, replenishing with boiling water as necessary. Stand pudding 5 minutes before turning onto serving plate.
5 Meanwhile, make syrup.
6 Pour hot syrup over pudding; serve hot.
syrup Stir ingredients in small saucepan over medium heat until smooth; bring to the boil. Reduce heat; simmer, uncovered, 2 minutes.

prep + cook time *1 hour 15 minutes* serves 6
nutritional count per serving *14.4g total fat (9g saturated fat); 1308kJ (313 cal); 42.6g carbohydrate; 4.4g protein; 0.9g fibre*

gluten-free desserts & cakes

SNACKS

HAM, ZUCCHINI AND CHIVE MUFFINS

Preheat oven to 200°C/180°C fan-forced. Grease 12-hole (⅓-cup/80ml) muffin pan. Whisk 80g melted butter, 1 egg and 1 cup buttermilk in large bowl. Stir in ½ cup finely chopped lean ham, ½ cup coarsely grated cheddar cheese, ¼ cup finely chopped fresh chives and 1 coarsely grated medium zucchini. Sift in 2 cups self-raising flour; mix gently (do not over-mix; mixture should be lumpy). Divide mixture into pan holes. Bake muffins about 20 minutes or until browned. Stand muffins 5 minutes before turning, top-side up, onto wire rack. Serve muffins warm.

prep + cook time *30 minutes* makes *12*
nutritional count per muffin *8.7g total fat (5.3g saturated fat); 769kJ (184 cal); 19g carbohydrate; 6.7g protein; 1.1g fibre*

FRUIT AND NUT TRAIL MIX

Combine ½ cup almond kernels, ½ cup brazil nuts, ¼ cup pecans, ¼ cup pepitas, ¼ cup sunflower seed kernels and ¼ cup dried goji berries in a small bowl. Store in an airtight container.

prep time *5 minutes* serves *6*
nutritional count per serving *26.9g total fat (3.5g saturated fat); 1275kJ (305 cal); 6.3g carbohydrate; 8.4g protein; 4.5g fibre*

Store fruit and nut mix in an airtight container, in the refrigerator, for up to 3 months.

SULTANA CINNAMON MINI MUFFINS

Preheat oven to 180°C/160°C fan-forced. Line two 12-hole (1-tablespoon/20ml) mini muffin pans with paper cases. Combine ¾ cup self-raising flour, ⅓ cup firmly packed brown sugar, ¼ cup rolled oats and ¼ cup sultanas in medium bowl. Whisk ½ cup milk, ¼ cup vegetable oil and 1 egg in small bowl; stir into dry ingredients (do not overmix; mixture should be lumpy). Divide mixture into paper cases. Bake about 15 minutes; turn, top-side up, onto wire rack. Combine 2 teaspoons caster sugar with ¼ teaspoon ground cinnamon; sprinkle over hot muffins.

prep + cook time *30 minutes* makes *24*
nutritional count per muffin *2.9g total fat (0.5g saturated fat); 268kJ (64 cal); 8.6g carbohydrate; 1.1g protein; 0.3g fibre*

GARLIC, ROSEMARY AND WHITE BEAN DIP

Rinse and drain 420g can white beans; process with ⅓ cup greek-style yogurt, 2 tablespoons lemon juice, 1 crushed garlic clove and ½ teaspoon finely chopped fresh rosemary until smooth. Season to taste. Serve with raw vegetable sticks.

prep time *10 minutes* serves *6*
nutritional count per serving *1.2g total fat (0.7g saturated fat); 222kJ (53 cal); 6.2g carbohydrate; 3.4g protein; 2.2g fibre*

snacks

CARAMELISED FIGS

Combine 1 cup low-fat yogurt, 2 teaspoons honey, ¼ teaspoon ground nutmeg, ¼ teaspoon ground cinnamon and pinch ground cloves in small bowl. Halve 6 large fresh figs lengthways; brush cut-side of figs with 1 tablespoon warm honey. Cook figs, cut-side down, in heated oiled large frying pan about 5 minutes or until browned lightly. Serve figs with spiced yogurt.

prep time + cook time *20 minutes* serves *4*
nutritional count per serving *0.5g total fat (0.1g saturated fat); 523kJ (125 cal); 22.6g carbohydrate; 5.8g protein; 3g fibre*

DRIED PEAR CRISPS

Preheat oven to 120°C/100°C fan-forced. Using mandolin or V-slicer, finely slice 1 medium pear lengthways. Place slices, in single layer, on wire rack over oven tray. Combine 1 teaspoon caster sugar with a pinch ground ginger and a pinch ground cinnamon; sprinkle over pear slices. Bake about 1 hour 20 minutes or until pear slices are dry and crisp.

prep + cook time *1 hour 30 minutes* makes *24*
nutritional count per crisp *0g total fat (0g saturated fat); 33kJ (8 cal); 1.9g carbohydrate; 0g protein; 0.2g fibre*

A firm pear, such as corella, is best for this recipe. The pear slices will become crisper when cool. The crisps are best eaten the day they are made.

GOJI MUESLI BARS

Preheat oven to 160°C/140°C fan-forced. Grease 20cm x 30cm lamington pan; line base and sides with baking paper, extending paper 2cm over long sides. Combine 125g chopped butter, ½ cup firmly packed brown sugar and 2 tablespoons honey in medium saucepan; stir over low heat until sugar dissolves. Transfer butter mixture to medium bowl; stir in 2¼ cups rolled oats, ½ cup dried goji berries (or blueberries or cranberries), ¼ cup sunflower seed kernels and ¼ cup desiccated coconut. Press mixture into pan; sprinkle with 2 tablespoons flaked almonds. Bake about 35 minutes. Cut into bars while still warm; cool in pan.

prep + cook time *45 minutes* makes 15
nutritional count per muesli bar *10.5g total fat
5.8g saturated fat); 786kJ (188 cal);
21g carbohydrate; 2.3g protein; 2g fibre*

CAPSICUM HUMMUS

Rinse and drain 400g can chickpeas; process with ¼ cup water, ⅓ cup coarsely chopped roasted red capsicum, ¼ cup tahini, 2 tablespoons lemon juice, 2 tablespoons olive oil and 1 crushed garlic clove until smooth. Season to taste. Serve with toasted wholemeal pitta triangles.

prep time *10 minutes* serves 6
nutritional count per serving *14.4g total fat
(1.9g saturated fat); 769kJ (184 cal);
6.8g carbohydrate; 5.4g protein; 3.9g fibre*

snacks

113

GLOSSARY

BARLEY nutritious grain used in soups and stews. Hulled barley, the least processed form, is high in fibre.

BEANS
black-eyed also known as black-eyed peas or cowpeas; not too dissimilar to white beans in flavour.
borlotti also known as roman beans or pink beans; can be eaten fresh or dried. Interchangeable with pinto beans because they're both pale pink or beige with dark red streaks.
broad also known as fava, windsor and horse beans. Fresh and frozen forms should be peeled twice, discarding both the outer long green pod and the beige-green tough inner shell.
butter also known as lima beans; large, flat, kidney-shaped bean, off-white in colour, with a mealy texture and mild taste.
cannellini small white bean similar in appearance and flavour to great northern, navy or haricot – all of which can be substituted for the other.
four-bean mix is made up of kidney, butter, cannellini beans and chickpeas.
kidney medium-sized red bean, slightly floury in texture yet sweet in flavour.
soya very nutritious; high in protein and low in carbohydrates, and the source of products such as tofu, soy milk, soy sauce, tamari and miso. Sometimes sold fresh as edamame. Also available dried and canned.
sprouts also known as bean shoots; tender new growths of assorted beans and seeds. The most readily available are mung bean, soya bean, alfalfa and snow pea sprouts.
white some recipes may simply call for "white beans", a generic term we use for canned or dried cannellini, haricot, navy or great northern beans.

BEETROOT also known as red beets or beets; firm, round root vegetable.

BICARBONATE OF SODA (also baking or carb soda); a mild alkali used as a leavening agent in baking.

BREADCRUMBS, PACKAGED fine-textured, crunchy, purchased white breadcrumbs.

BUCKWHEAT a herb in the same plant family as rhubarb; not a cereal so it is gluten-free. Available as flour; ground (cracked) into coarse, medium or fine grain; or as groats, the roasted whole kernels cooked similarly to rice or couscous.

BUK CHOY also known as bok choy, pak choi, chinese white cabbage or chinese chard; has a fresh, mild mustard taste.

BURGHUL also known as bulghur or bulgar wheat; hulled steamed wheat kernels that, once dried, are crushed into various size grains. Not the same as cracked wheat. Found in most supermarkets or health-food stores.

BUTTER use salted or unsalted (sweet) butter; 125g is equal to one stick (4 ounces) of butter.

BUTTERMILK originally the term given to the slightly sour liquid left after butter was churned from cream, today it is commercially made similarly to yogurt. Sold alongside all fresh milk products in supermarkets; despite the implication of its name, it is low in fat.

CARDAMOM the pods are the fruit of a large ginger-like plant that's native to the rainforests of southern India; available in pod, seed or ground form. Has an aromatic, sweetly rich flavour, and is one of the world's most expensive spices.

CHEESE
cheddar the most widely eaten cheese in the world, cheddar is a semi-hard cow's-milk cheese.
cottage fresh, white, unripened curd cheese with a grainy consistency.
fetta a crumbly goat's- or sheep's-milk cheese with a sharp salty taste.
goat's made from goat's milk, has an earthy, strong taste; available in both soft and firm textures, in various shapes and sizes and sometimes rolled in ash or herbs.
parmesan also known as parmigiano; a hard, grainy cow's-milk cheese. The curd is salted in brine for a month before being aged for up to two years in humid conditions.

ricotta a soft, white, cow's-milk cheese. The name roughly translates as "cooked again". Made from whey, a by-product of other cheese-making, to which fresh milk and acid are added. Ricotta is a sweet, moist cheese with a slightly grainy texture.

CHICKPEAS also called garbanzos, hummus or channa; an irregularly round, sandy-coloured legume.

CHILLI available in many different types and sizes. Use rubber gloves when seeding and chopping fresh chillies as they can burn your skin. Removing seeds and membranes lessens the heat level.
FLAKES deep-red, dehydrated chilli slices and whole seeds.
green any unripened chilli; also some varieties that are ripe when green.
long red available both fresh and dried; a generic term used for any moderately hot, long (6cm-8cm), thin chilli.
red thai small, hot and bright red in colour.

CHINESE COOKING WINE also known as hao hsing or chinese rice wine; made from fermented rice. It is available from Asian food stores and most major supermarkets. Dry sherry is an adequate substitute.

CHIVES related to the onion and leek, with a subtle onion flavour.

CHOCOLATE, DARK EATING also known as semi-sweet or luxury chocolate; made of a high percentage of cocoa liquor and cocoa butter, and a little added sugar.

CHOY SUM also known as pakaukeo or flowering cabbage, a member of the buk choy family; easy to identify with its long stems, light green leaves and yellow flowers. Is eaten, stems and all, steamed or stir-fried.

CINNAMON dried inner bark of the shoots of the cinnamon tree; available in stick (quill) or ground form.

CLOVES dried flower buds of a tropical tree; can be used whole or in ground form. Has a distinctively pungent and "spicy" scent and flavour.

COCOA POWDER also known as cocoa; dried, unsweetened, roasted, ground cocoa beans (cacao seeds).

COCONUT
cream obtained commercially from the first pressing of the coconut flesh alone, without the addition of water. Available from supermarkets.
desiccated unsweetened, dried, finely shredded concentrated coconut.

CORIANDER also known as pak chee, cilantro or chinese parsley; bright-green leafy herb with a pungent flavour. Both the stems and roots are also used in cooking; wash well before using. Also available ground, or as seeds; do not substitute for fresh coriander as the tastes are completely different.

CORN, BABY immature sweetcorn. Available fresh and frozen from most supermarkets and greengrocers.

CORNFLOUR (cornstarch); used as a thickening agent. Available as 100% maize (corn) and wheaten cornflour.

CRANBERRIES, DRIED have the same slightly sour, succulent flavour as fresh cranberries. Available in most supermarkets and health-food stores.

CUMIN also known as zeera or comino; a spice with a spicy, nutty flavour.

EGGPLANT purple-skinned vegetable also known as aubergine.

FISH FILLETS, FIRM WHITE ling, blue eye, bream, flathead, swordfish, whiting, jewfish, snapper or sea perch are all good choices. Check for any small pieces of bone in the fillets and use tweezers to remove them.

FLOUR
brown rice retains the outer bran layer of the rice grain.
buckwheat not a true cereal, but flour is made from its seeds. Available from health-food stores.
plain all-purpose flour made from wheat. Also available gluten-free from most supermarkets.
potato made from cooked potatoes that have been dried and ground.
rice very fine, almost powdery, gluten-free flour; made from ground white rice.

self-raising plain flour mixed with baking powder in the proportion of 1 cup flour to 2 teaspoons baking powder. Also available gluten-free from most supermarkets.
soya made from ground soya beans.
spelt very similar to wheat, but has a slightly nuttier, sweeter flavour. Spelt has gluten, just like wheat, so is not suitable for a gluten-free diet.

GARAM MASALA a blend of spices based on cardamom, cinnamon, cloves, coriander, fennel and cumin, roasted and ground together. Black pepper and chilli can be added for more heat.

GELATINE we use powdered gelatine. It is also available in sheet form, known as leaf gelatine.

GINGER also known as green or root ginger; the thick root of a tropical plant.
ground or powdered ginger; used as a flavouring in cakes, etc, but cannot be substituted for fresh ginger.

GOJI BERRIES originated around Tibet/Inner Mongolia. The small red berries grow on a type of shrub. While often eaten dried, goji berries can be eaten straight from the vine. They are very juicy and have a sweet, delicious flavour. Available from health-food stores and some larger supermarkets.

GOLDEN SYRUP a by-product of refined sugarcane; pure maple syrup or honey can be substituted.

GRAPEFRUIT the largest available citrus fruit, grapefruit are available with or without seeds; the seeded variety has more flavour. The pink version is called ruby grapefruit.

KECAP MANIS see *sauces*.

LEEK a member of the onion family, resembles a green onion but is much larger and more subtle and mild in flavour.

LENTILS green lentils tend to hold their shaped better than other lentils when cooked. Australian green lentils are available from speciality food stores, health-food stores and some supermarkets. They are also known as french green or matilda lentils.

MAPLE SYRUP a thin syrup distilled from the sap of the maple tree. Maple-flavoured syrup or pancake syrup is not an adequate substitute for the real thing.

MILK
reduced-fat contains less than or equal to 2 per cent fat and may have extra protein and calcium added.
rice usually made from filtered water and brown rice. It has less protein and calcium than cow's milk, but is high in carbohydrates and contains no lactose or cholesterol. Is not as thick as dairy or soy milks, and has a somewhat translucent consistency and a slightly sweet flavour.
soy a rich, creamy, gluten-free "milk" extracted from soya beans that have been crushed in hot water and strained. It has a nutty flavour. Sometimes malt and barley extract are added to soy milk to make it more palatable. Ensure you use gluten-free soy milk if you have a gluten allergy.

MINCE also known as ground meat.

MIRIN a champagne-coloured cooking wine; made of glutinous rice and alcohol and only used for cooking. Should not be confused with sake.

MISO Japan's famous bean paste made from fermented soya beans. It varies in colour, texture and saltiness. The darker the miso is, the longer it has fermented and the more intense and mature its taste. Red miso is a combination of barley and soya beans. Miso should be kept in the refrigerator where it lasts for six months. It is available from Asian food stores and some major supermarkets.

MUSHROOMS
flat large, flat mushrooms with a rich, earthy flavour. They are sometimes misnamed field mushrooms, which are wild mushrooms.
shiitake, dried are also known as donko or dried chinese mushrooms; rehydrate before use.

MUSTARD
dijon a pale brown, distinctively flavoured, fairly mild french mustard.

seeds available in black, brown or yellow varieties; brown seeds are more spicy and piquant than yellow or white. Available from health-food stores and some major supermarkets.

NUTMEG the dried nut of an evergreen tree native to Indonesia; it is available in ground form or you can grate your own with a fine grater.

OIL
cooking-oil spray we use an oil spray made from cholesterol-free canola oil.
flaxseed also known as linseed oil. Extracted from the seeds of the flax plant. Must be refrigerated once opened, and used within 3-6 weeks.
macadamia extracted from crushed macadamia nuts.
olive made from ripened olives. Extra virgin and virgin are the best, while extra light or light refers to taste, not fat levels.
peanut pressed from ground peanuts; has a high smoke point (capacity to handle high heat without burning).
sesame made from roasted, crushed, white sesame seeds; a flavouring rather than a cooking medium.
vegetable sourced from plants rather than animal fats.

PAPRIKA ground, dried, sweet red capsicum (bell pepper); there are many types available, including mild, sweet, hot and smoked.

PEPITAS edible dried pumpkin seeds that have had their white hull removed. They are green, and have a delicate nutty flavour.

PINE NUTS also known as pignoli; not, in fact, a nut but a small, cream-coloured kernel from pine cones.

PRAWNS also known as shrimp.

PUFFED CEREALS rice, corn and millet that have been steamed then heated until they puff up. Found in health-food stores.

RICE FLAKES flattened grains of rice; available from health-food shops and most supermarkets.

RICE, SHORT-GRAIN fat, almost round grain with a high starch content; tends to clump together when cooked.

SAKE rice wine used in cooking or as a drink. If unavailable, substitute dry sherry or brandy.

SASHIMI SALMON use the freshest, sashimi-quality fish you can find. Raw fish sold as sashimi has to meet stringent guidelines regarding its handling and treatment after leaving the water. We suggest you seek local advice from authorities before eating any raw seafood.

SAUCES
fish also called nam pla or nuoc nam; made from pulverised salted fermented fish, most often anchovies. Has a pungent smell and strong taste, so use sparingly.
hoisin a thick, sweet and spicy Chinese sauce made from salted fermented soya beans, onions and garlic.
oyster Asian in origin, this rich, brown sauce is made from oysters and their brine, cooked with salt and soy sauce, and thickened with starches.
soy also known as sieu; is made from fermented soya beans. There are several variations available in supermarkets and Asian food stores. We use japanese soy unless indicated otherwise. It is an all-purpose low-sodium soy sauce made with more wheat content than its Chinese counterparts; it is the best table soy, and the one to choose if you only want one variety.
kecap manis a dark, thick sweet soy sauce with added molasses or palm sugar for sweetness.
light a fairly thin, pale sauce; used in dishes in which the natural colour of the ingredients is to be maintained. Is the saltiest tasting of all, and should not be confused with salt-reduced or low-sodium soy sauces.
tamari a thick, dark soy sauce made mainly from soya beans without the wheat used in standard soy sauces.
sweet chilli a comparatively mild, Thai-type sauce made from red chillies, sugar, garlic and vinegar.
tomato pasta a prepared sauce made from tomatoes, herbs and spices.

SNOW PEAS also called mange tout ("eat all").

SUGAR
brown soft, fine sugar retaining molasses for its colour and flavour.
caster also known as superfine or finely granulated table sugar.
icing also known as confectioners' sugar or powdered sugar; granulated sugar crushed together with a small amount of cornflour.
palm also known as nam tan pip, jawa, jaggery or gula melaka; made from the sap of the sugar palm tree. Light brown to black in colour and usually sold in rock-hard cakes. If unavailable, substitute with brown sugar.
pure icing also known as confectioners' sugar or powdered sugar, but has no added cornflour.
white a coarsely granulated table sugar, also known as crystal sugar.

SUGAR SNAP PEAS also known as honey snap peas; fresh small pea that can be eaten whole, pod and all, similarly to snow peas.

SULTANAS dried grapes, also known as golden raisins.

SUNFLOWER SEED KERNELS are dried husked sunflower seeds.

TAHINI a rich sesame-seed paste available from Middle-Eastern food stores and many supermarkets.

TAMARI *see sauces.*

TOFU also known as bean curd, an off-white, custard-like product made from the "milk" of crushed soya beans; comes fresh as soft or firm. Leftover fresh tofu can be refrigerated in water (which is changed daily) for 4 days.
firm tofu made by compressing bean curd to remove most of the water. Good used in stir-fries because it can be tossed without falling apart.
silken tofu refers to the method by which it is made, where it is strained through silk.

TURMERIC, GROUND a member of the ginger family; its root is dried and ground, resulting in the rich yellow powder that gives many Indian dishes their characteristic yellow colour. It is intensely pungent in taste but not hot.

VANILLA EXTRACT vanilla beans that have been submerged in alcohol.

VINEGAR
balsamic originally from Modena, Italy; made from the juice of Trebbiano grapes. It is a deep rich brown colour with a sweet and sour flavour.
red wine based on fermented red wine.
rice a colourless vinegar made from fermented rice and flavoured with sugar and salt. Also known as seasoned rice vinegar.
rice wine made from rice wine lees (sediment), salt and alcohol.
white wine made from a blend of white wines.

WASABI (japanese horseradish) is available as a paste in tubes, or powdered in tins from Asian food stores and larger supermarkets.

WHEAT GERM is the reproductive area, or embryo, from which the seed germinates to form the sprout that becomes wheat. The term "germ" comes from the word germinate. It has a nutty flavour and is very oily, which causes it to turn rancid quickly. Wheat germ is usually separated from the bran and starch during the milling of flour because the germ's perishable oil content limits the keeping time of the flour. Available from health-food stores.

YEAST a 7g (¼oz) sachet of dried yeast (2 teaspoons) is equal to 15g (½oz) compressed yeast if substituting one for the other.

CONVERSION CHART

MEASURES

One Australian metric measuring cup holds approximately 250ml; one Australian metric tablespoon holds 20ml; one Australian metric teaspoon holds 5ml.

The difference between one country's measuring cups and another's is within a two- or three-teaspoon variance, and will not affect your cooking results. North America, New Zealand and the United Kingdom use a 15ml tablespoon.

All cup and spoon measurements are level. The most accurate way of measuring dry ingredients is to weigh them. When measuring liquids, use a clear glass or plastic jug with the metric markings.

We use large eggs with an average weight of 60g.

DRY MEASURES

METRIC	IMPERIAL
15g	½oz
30g	1oz
60g	2oz
90g	3oz
125g	4oz (¼lb)
155g	5oz
185g	6oz
220g	7oz
250g	8oz (½lb)
280g	9oz
315g	10oz
345g	11oz
375g	12oz (¾lb)
410g	13oz
440g	14oz
470g	15oz
500g	16oz (1lb)
750g	24oz (1½lb)
1kg	32oz (2lb)

LIQUID MEASURES

METRIC	IMPERIAL
30ml	1 fluid oz
60ml	2 fluid oz
100ml	3 fluid oz
125ml	4 fluid oz
150ml	5 fluid oz (¼ pint/1 gill)
190ml	6 fluid oz
250ml	8 fluid oz
300ml	10 fluid oz (½ pint)
500ml	16 fluid oz
600ml	20 fluid oz (1 pint)
1000ml (1 litre)	1¾ pints

LENGTH MEASURES

METRIC	IMPERIAL
3mm	⅛in
6mm	¼in
1cm	½in
2cm	¾in
2.5cm	1in
5cm	2in
6cm	2½in
8cm	3in
10cm	4in
13cm	5in
15cm	6in
18cm	7in
20cm	8in
23cm	9in
25cm	10in
28cm	11in
30cm	12in (1ft)

OVEN TEMPERATURES

These oven temperatures are only a guide for conventional ovens. For fan-forced ovens, check the manufacturer's manual.

	°C (CELSIUS)	°F (FAHRENHEIT)	GAS MARK
Very slow	120	250	½
Slow	150	275-300	1-2
Moderately slow	160	325	3
Moderate	180	350-375	4-5
Moderately hot	200	400	6
Hot	220	425-450	7-8
Very hot	240	475	9

INDEX

If you like this cookbook, you'll love these...

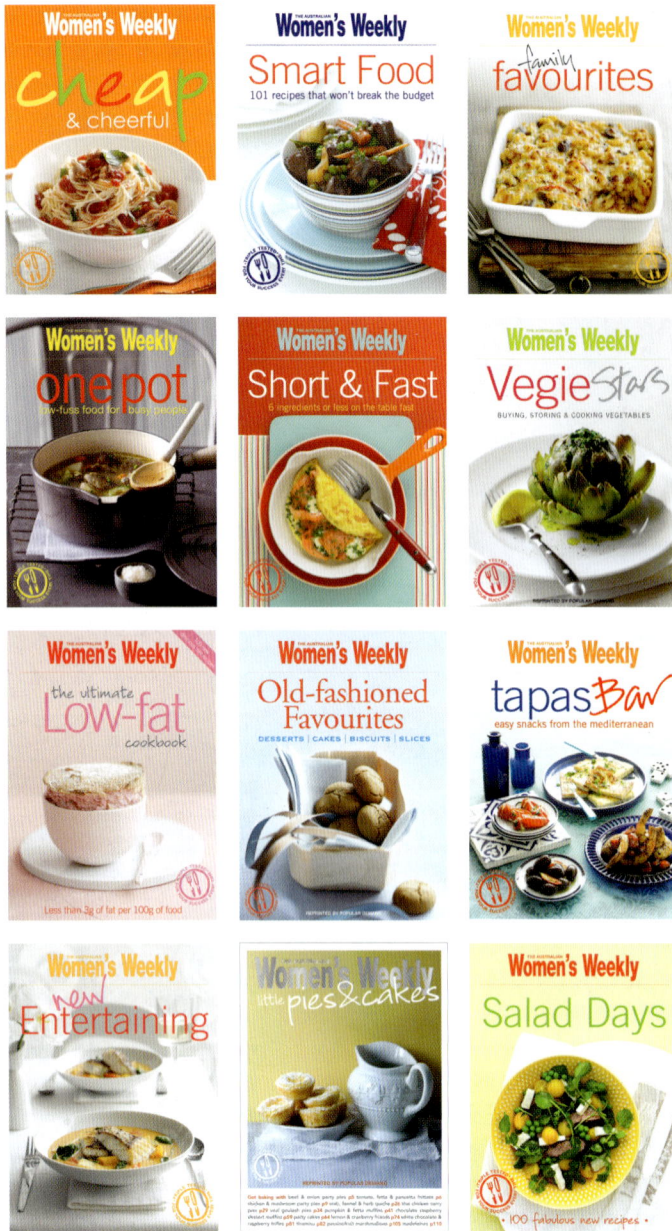

These are just a small selection of titles available in *The Australian Women's Weekly* range on sale at selected newsagents, supermarkets or online at www.acpbooks.com.au

also available in bookstores...

ACP BOOKS

General manager Christine Whiston
Editor-in-chief Susan Tomnay
Creative director & designer Hieu Chi Nguyen
Art director Hannah Blackmore
Senior editor Wendy Bryant
Food director Pamela Clark
Food writer Xanthe Roberts
Additional text Jordanna Levin
Nutritional information Nicole Jennings
Recipe development Kate Nichols, Rebecca Squadrito, Nicole Jennings
Sales & rights director Brian Cearnes
Marketing manager Bridget Cody
Senior business analyst Rebecca Varela
Circulation manager Jama Mclean
Operations manager David Scotto
Production manager Victoria Jefferys

ACP Books are published by ACP Magazines a division of PBL Media Pty Limited
PBL Media, Chief Executive Officer Ian Law
Publishing & sales director, Women's lifestyle Lynette Phillips
General manager, Editorial projects, Women's lifestyle Deborah Thomas
Editor at Large, Women's lifestyle Pat Ingram
Marketing director, Women's lifestyle Matthew Dominello
Commercial manager, Women's lifestyle Seymour Cohen
Research director, Women's lifestyle Justin Stone

Produced by ACP Books, Sydney.

Published by ACP Books, a division of ACP Magazines Ltd, 54 Park St, Sydney; GPO Box 4088, Sydney, NSW 2001. phone (02) 9282 8618; fax (02) 9267 9438. acpbooks@acpmagazines.com.au; www.acpbooks.com.au

Printed by Toppan Printing Co, China.

Australia Distributed by Network Services, phone +61 2 9282 8777; fax +61 2 9264 3278; networkweb@networkservicescompany.com.au

United Kingdom Distributed by Australian Consolidated Press (UK), phone (01604) 642 200; fax (01604) 642 300; books@acpuk.com

New Zealand Distributed by Netlink Distribution Company, phone (9) 366 9966; ask@ndc.co.nz

South Africa Distributed by PSD Promotions, phone (27 11) 392 6065/6/7; fax (27 11) 392 6079/80; orders@psdprom.co.za

Canada Distributed by Publishers Group Canada phone (800) 663 5714; fax (800) 565 3770; service@raincoast.com

Title: Super diet / food director Pamela Clark.
ISBN: 978 1 86396 864 5 (pbk.)
Notes: Includes index.
Subjects: Reducing diets – Recipes. Low-calorie diet – Recipes. Low-cholesterol diet – Recipes. Low-fat diet – Recipes. Cookery.
Other Authors/Contributors: Clark, Pamela.
Dewey Number: 641.5635

© ACP Magazines Ltd 2010
ABN 18 053 273 546
This publication is copyright. No part of it may be reproduced or transmitted in any form without the written permission of the publishers.

Scanpan cookware is used in the AWW Test Kitchen.

Photographer Julie Crespel **Stylist** Kate Brown
Food preparation Rebecca Squadrito; Liz Macri
Cover Crêpes with cranberry orange sauce, page 106

To order books, phone 136 116 (within Australia)
or order online at www.acpbooks.com.au
Send recipe enquiries to:
recipeenquiries@acpmagazines.com.au

acp books